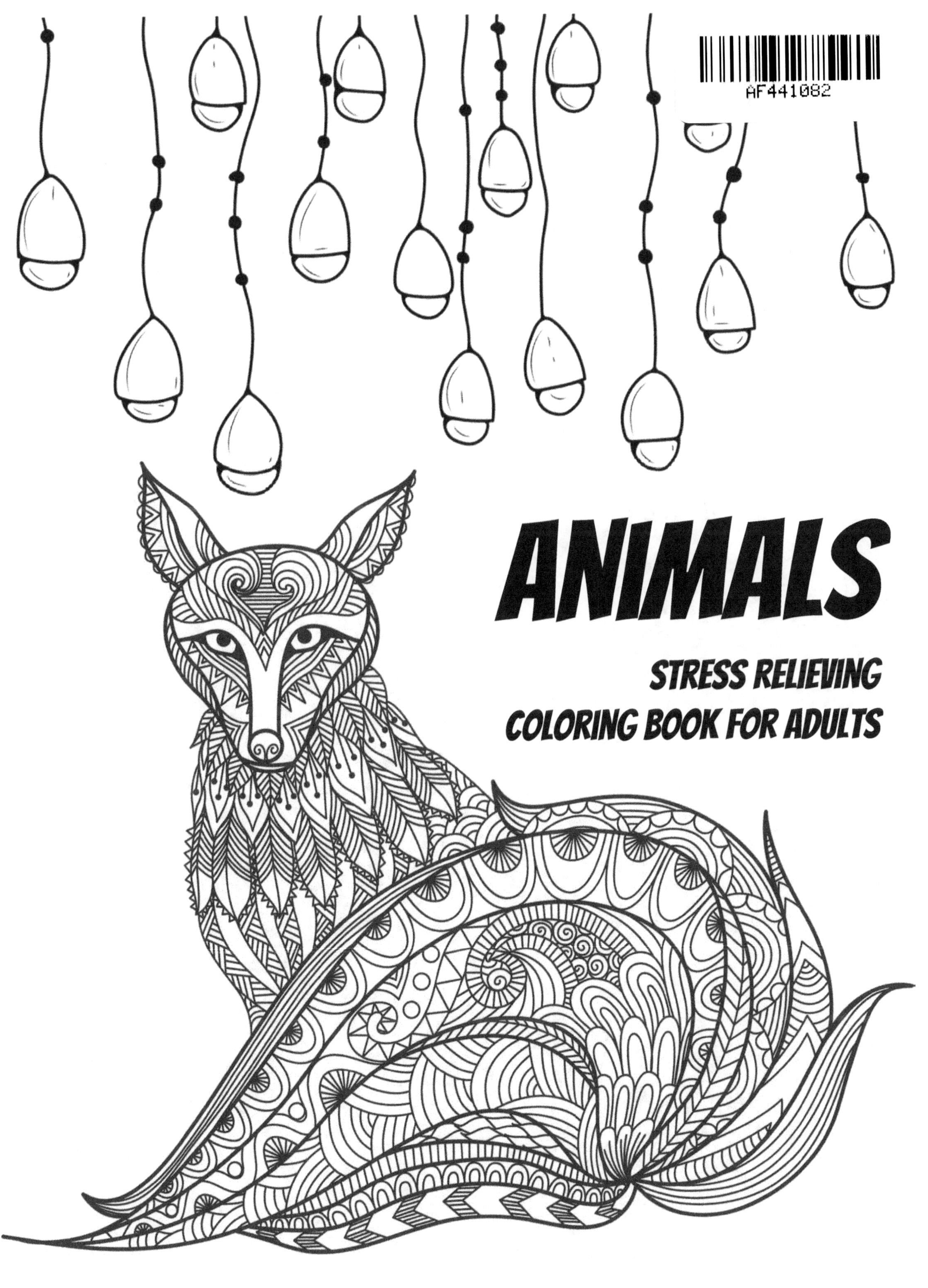
AF441082
ANIMALS
STRESS RELIEVING
COLORING BOOK FOR ADULTS

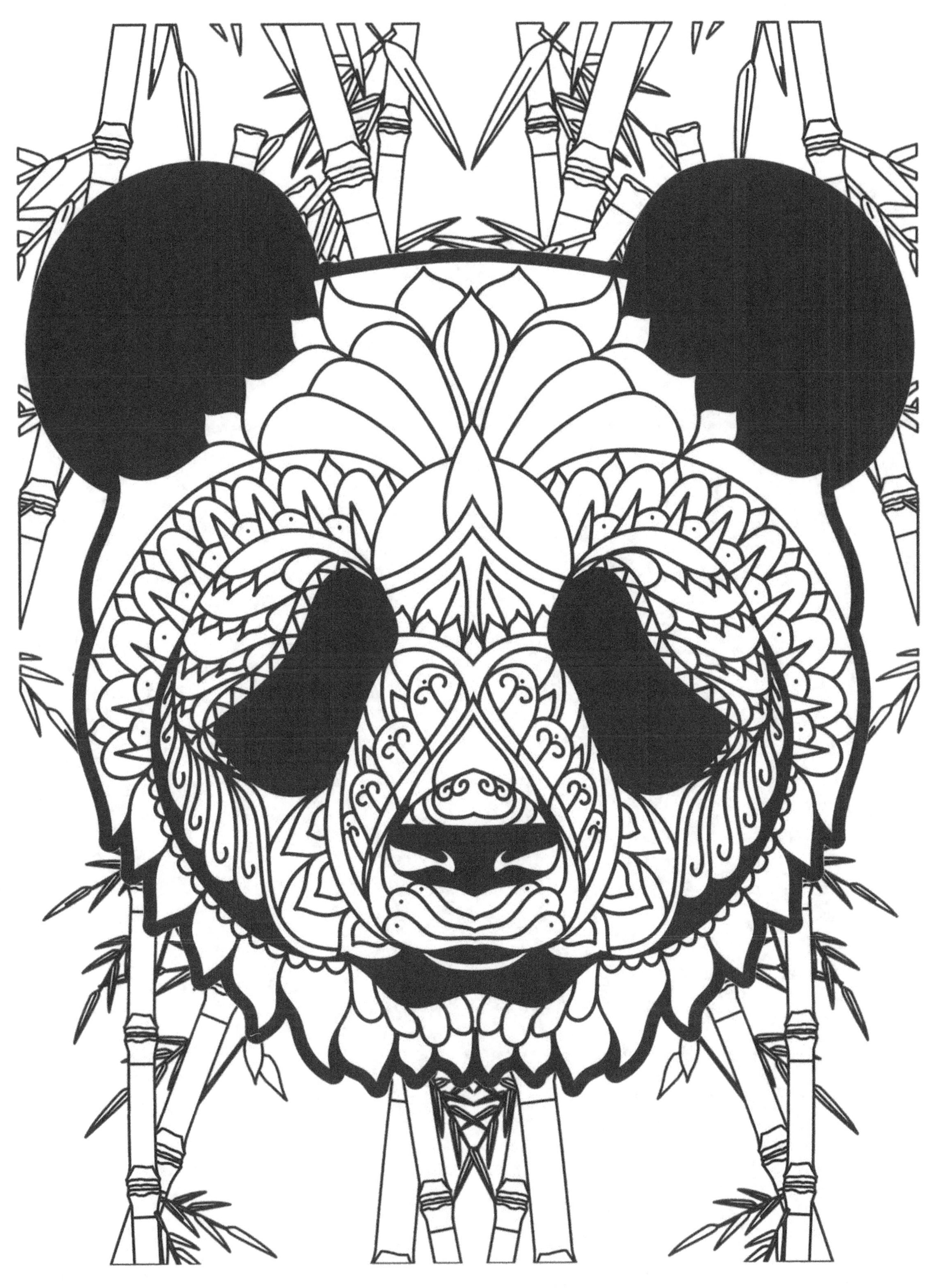

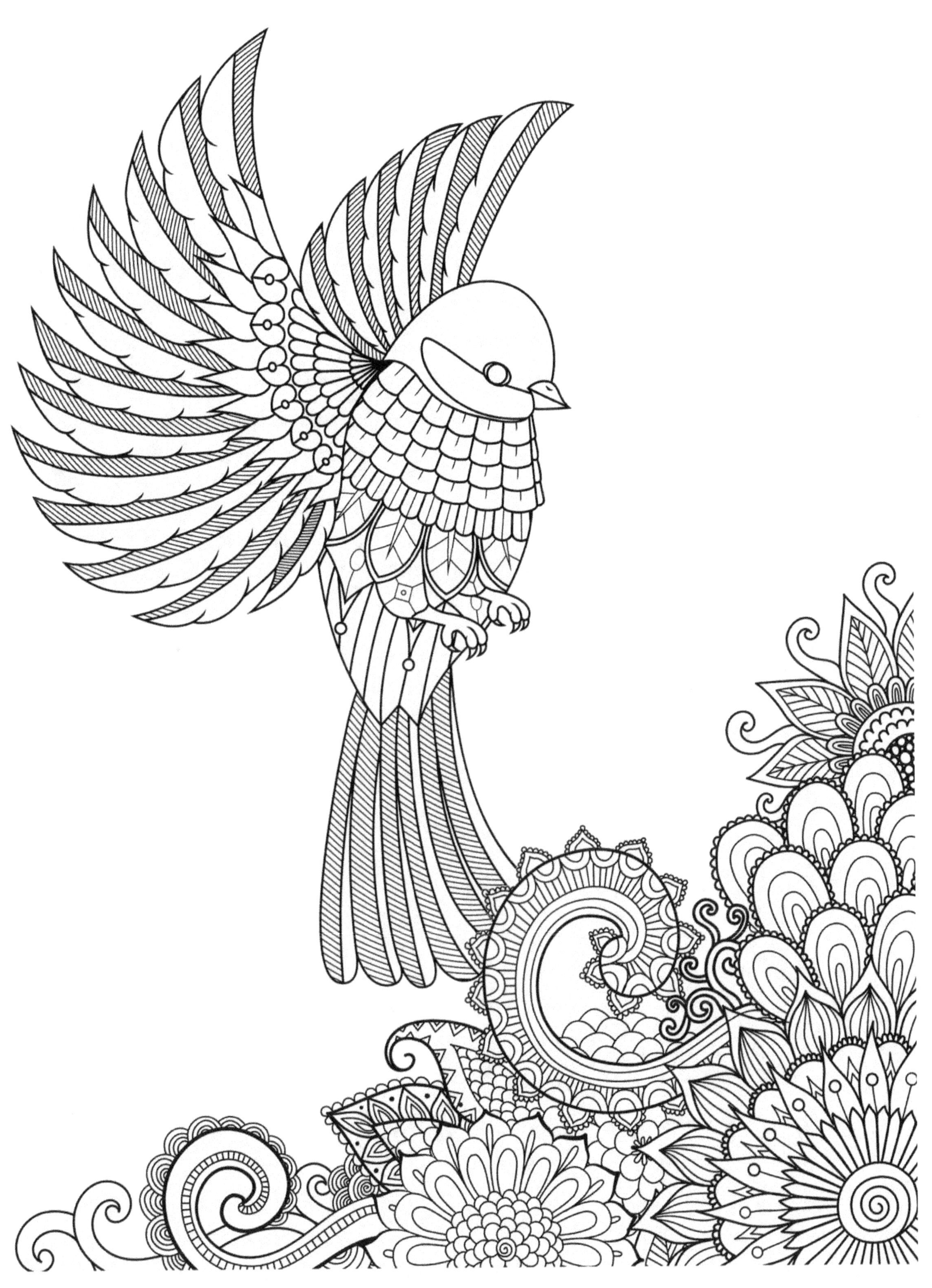

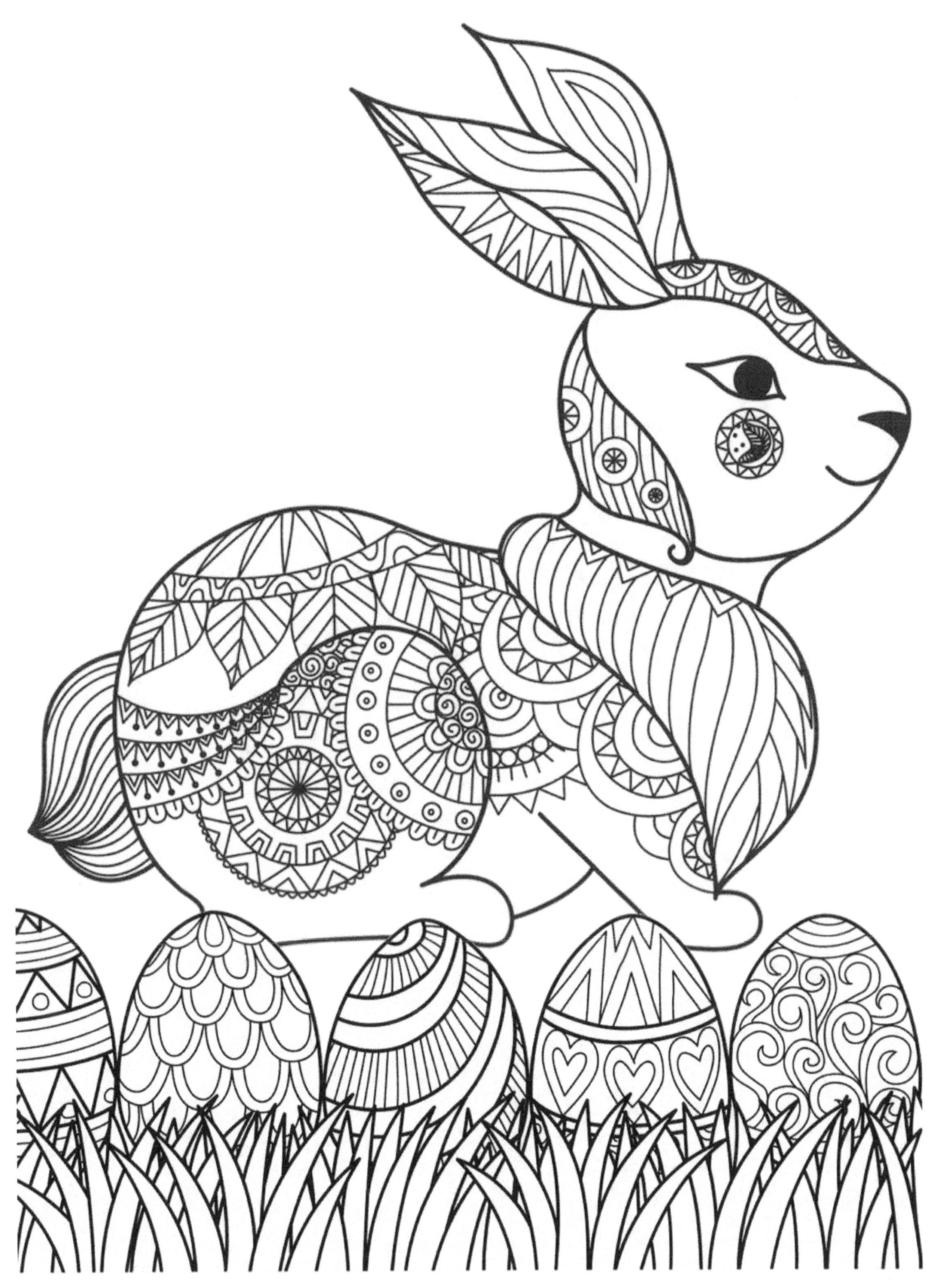

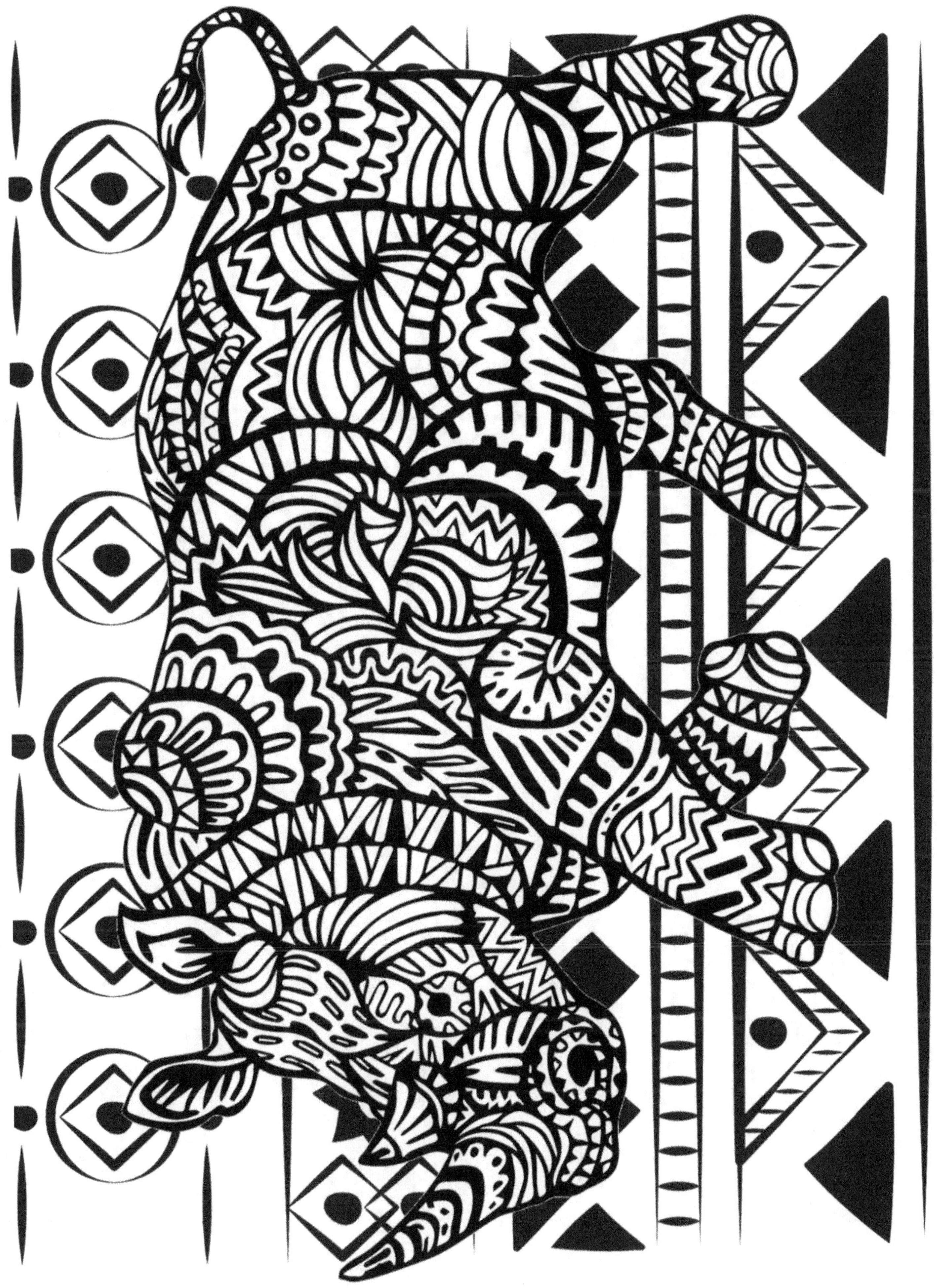

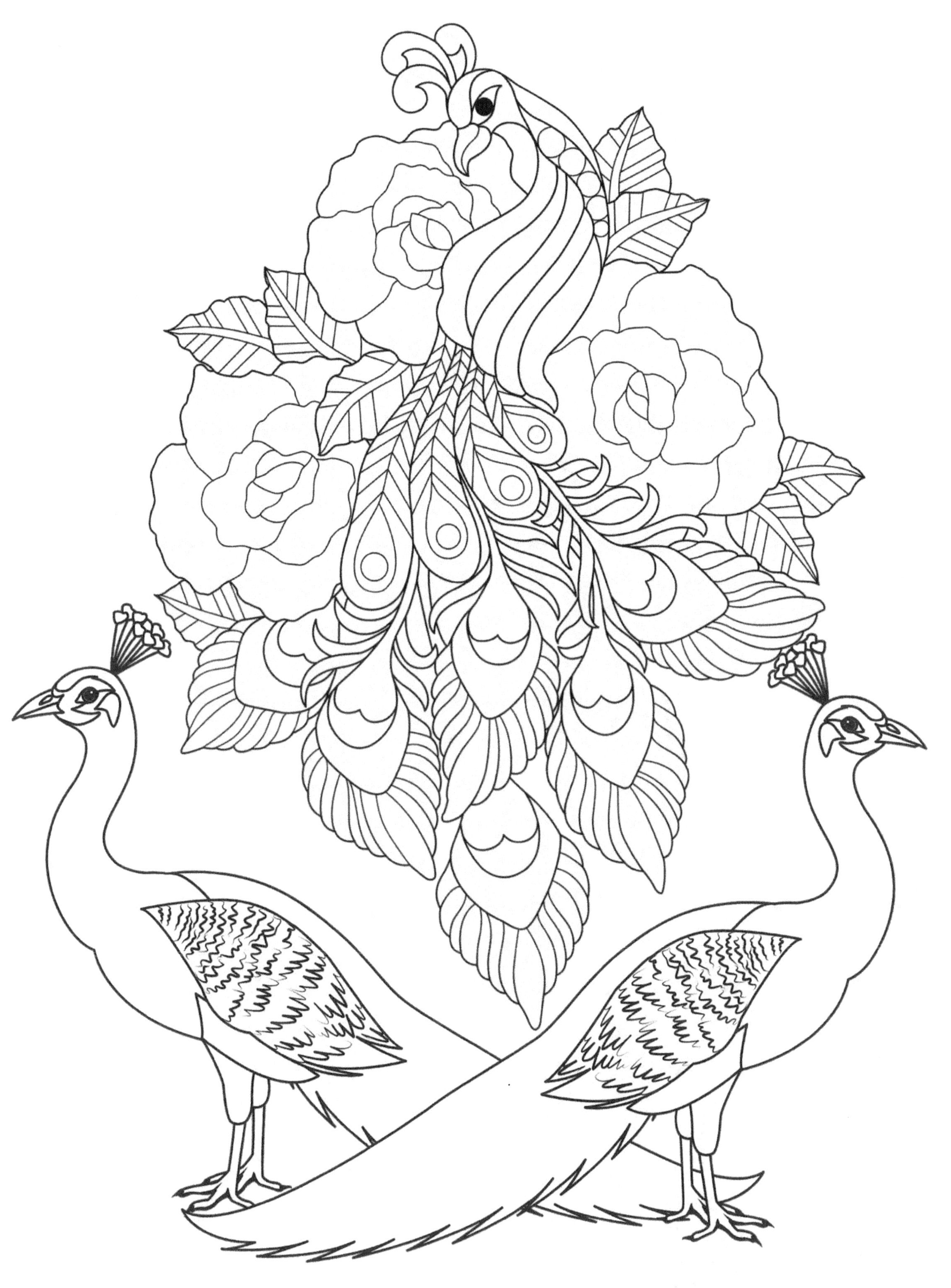

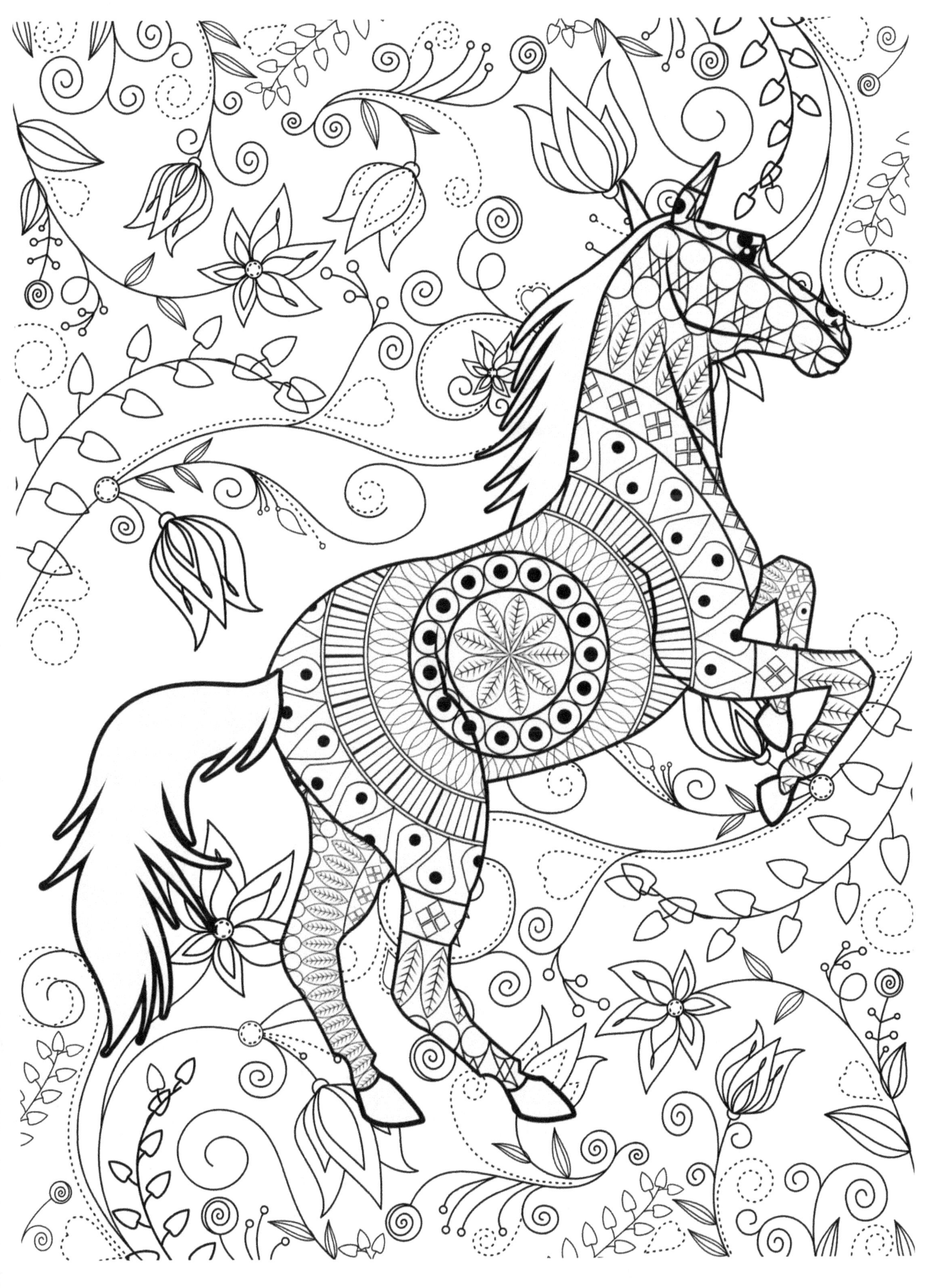

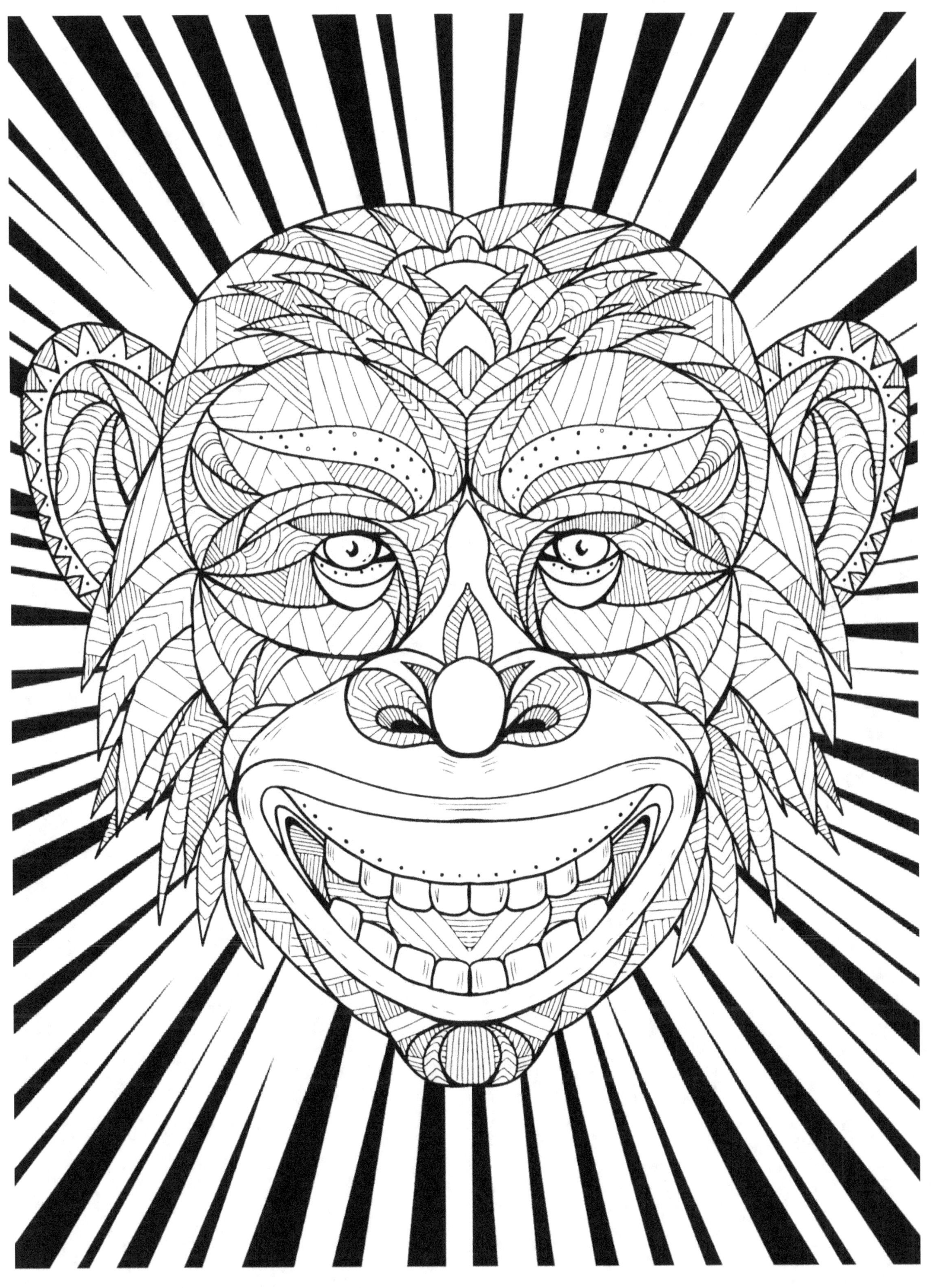

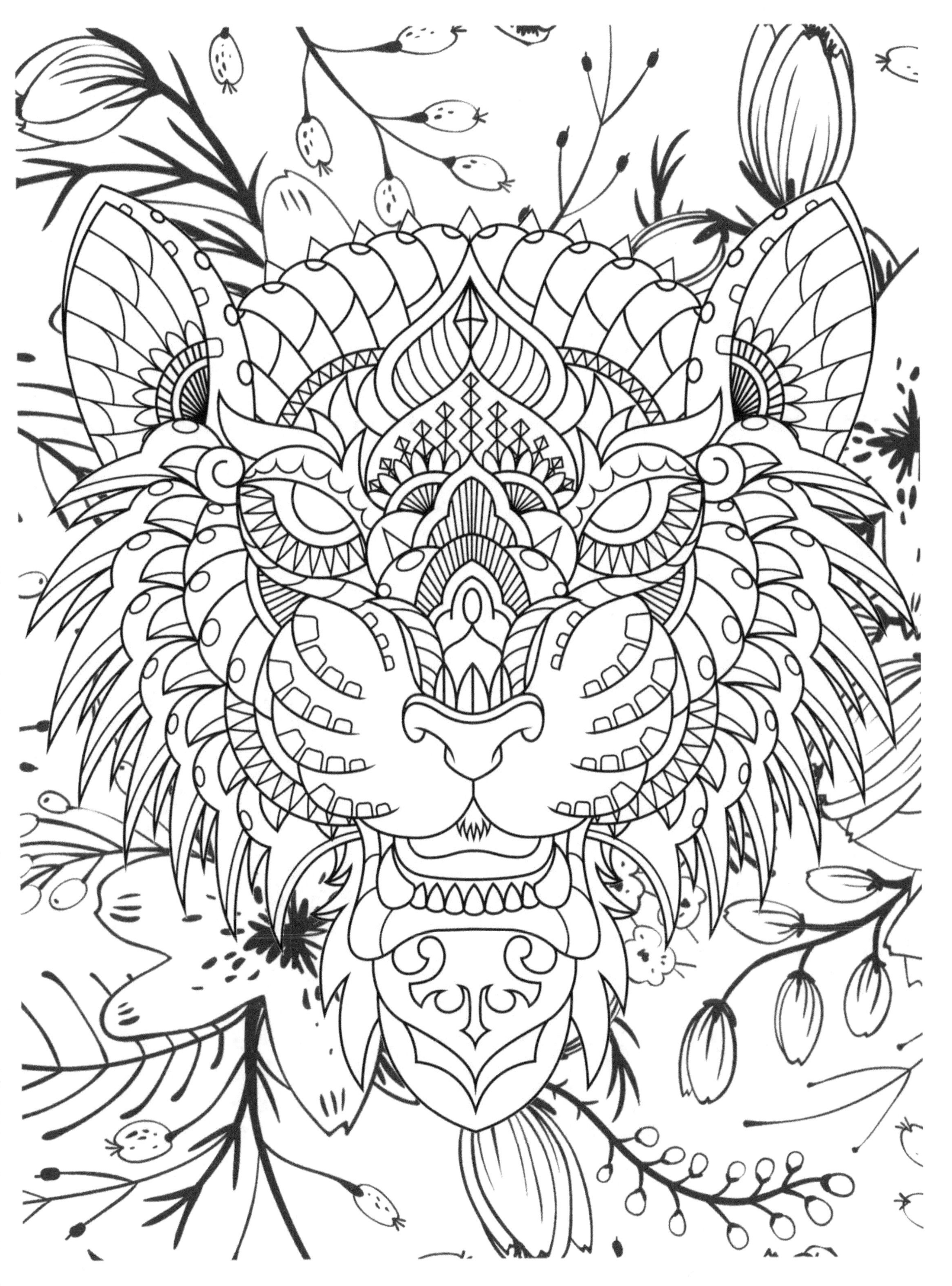

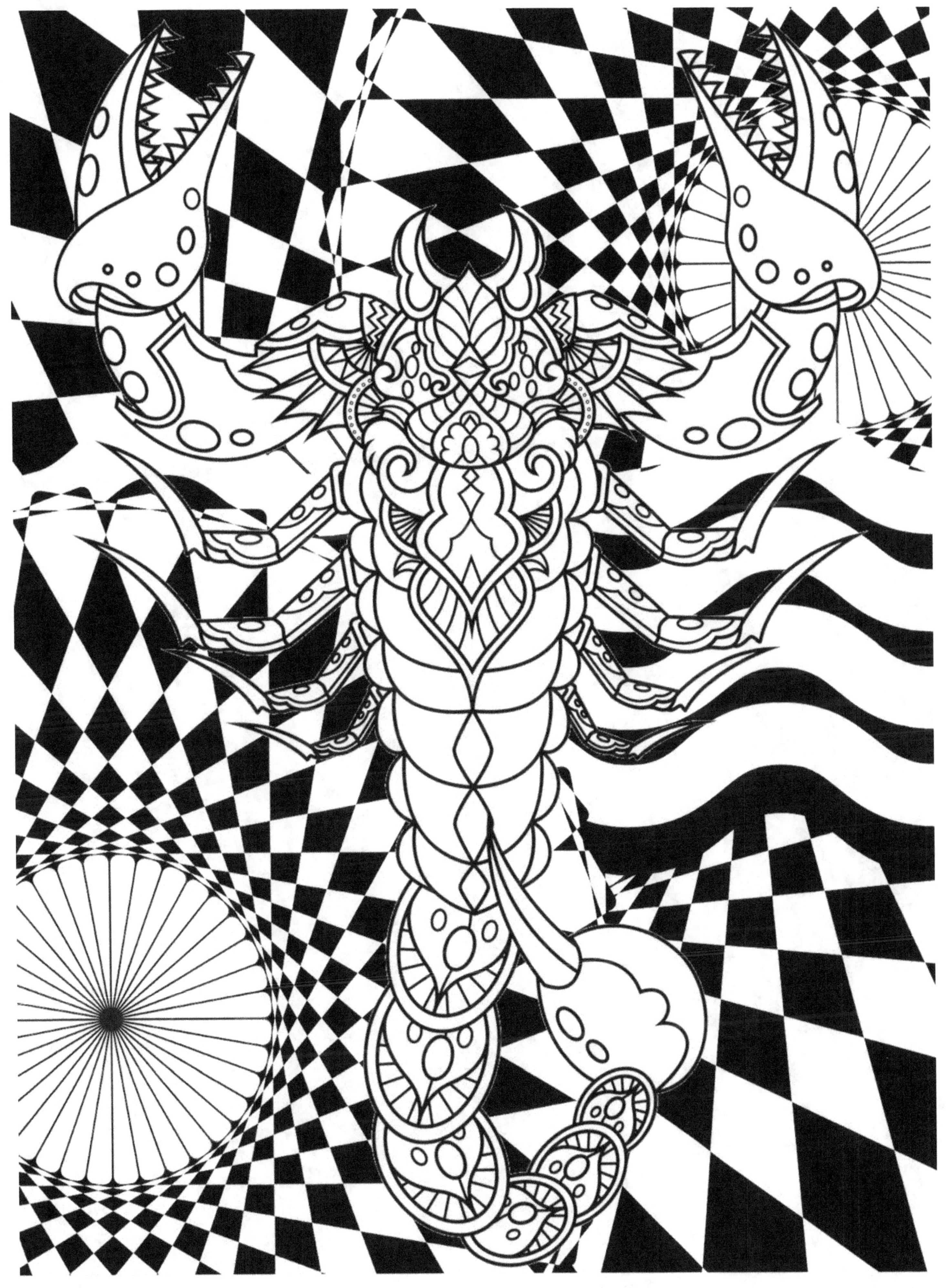

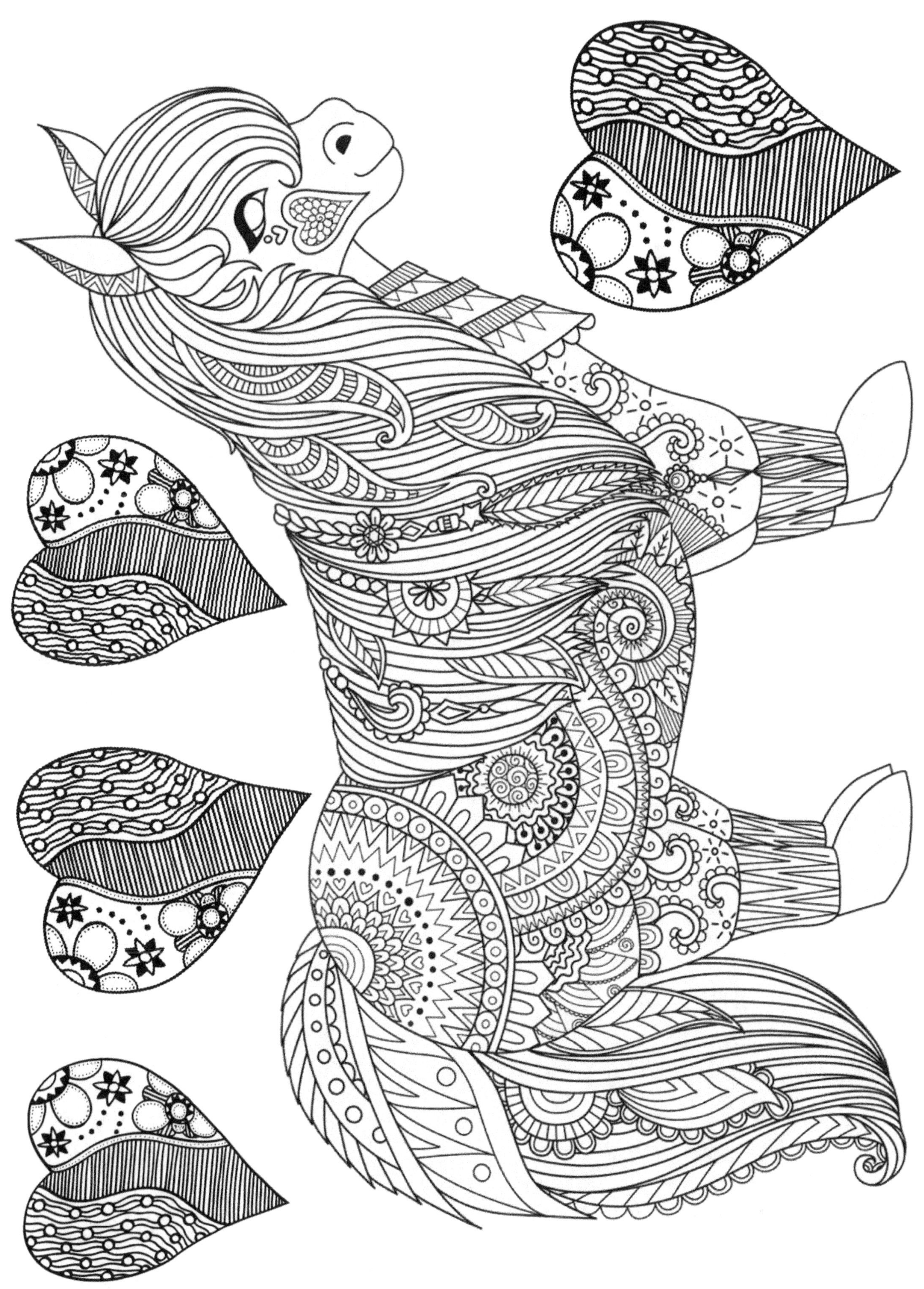

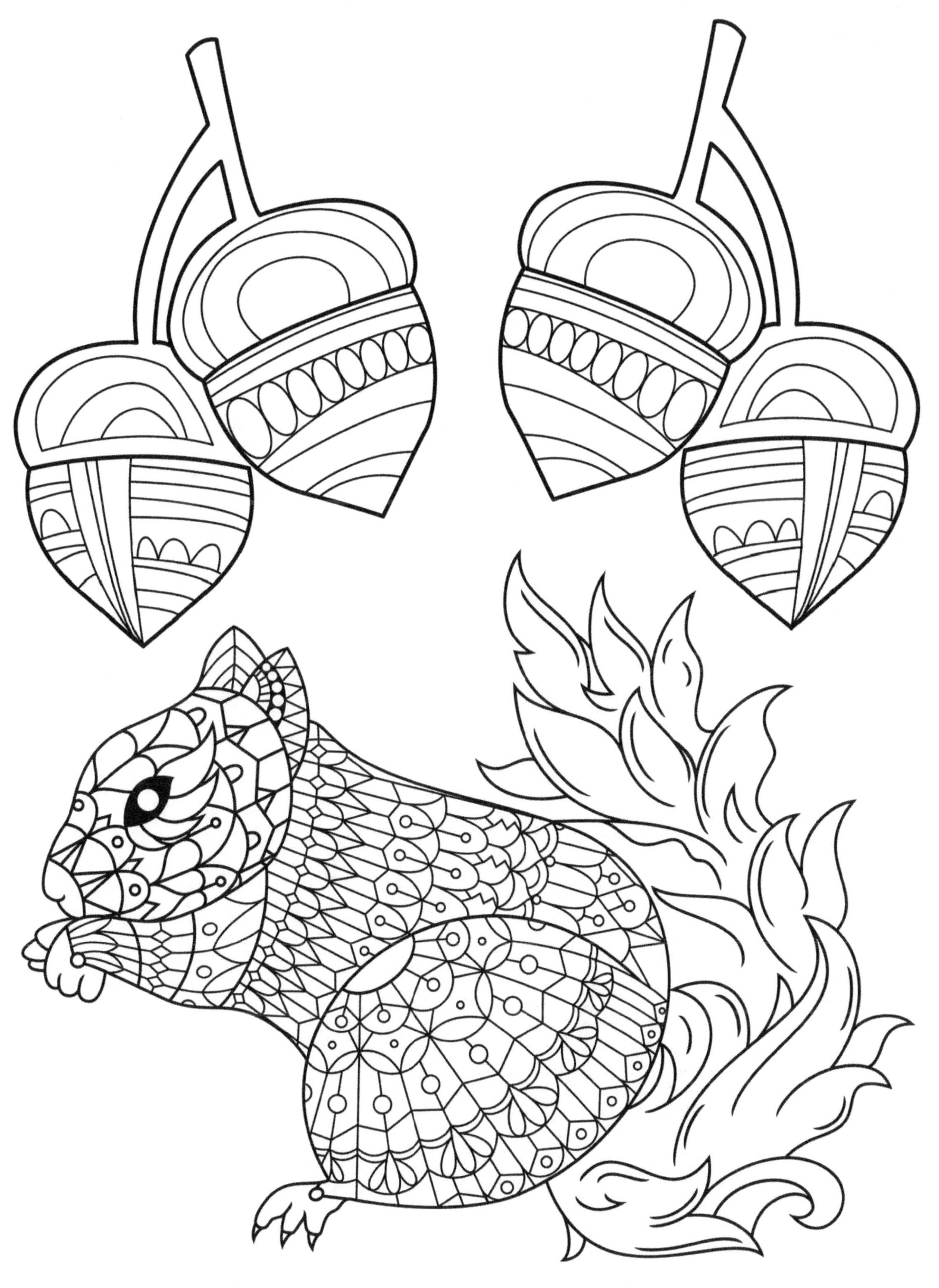

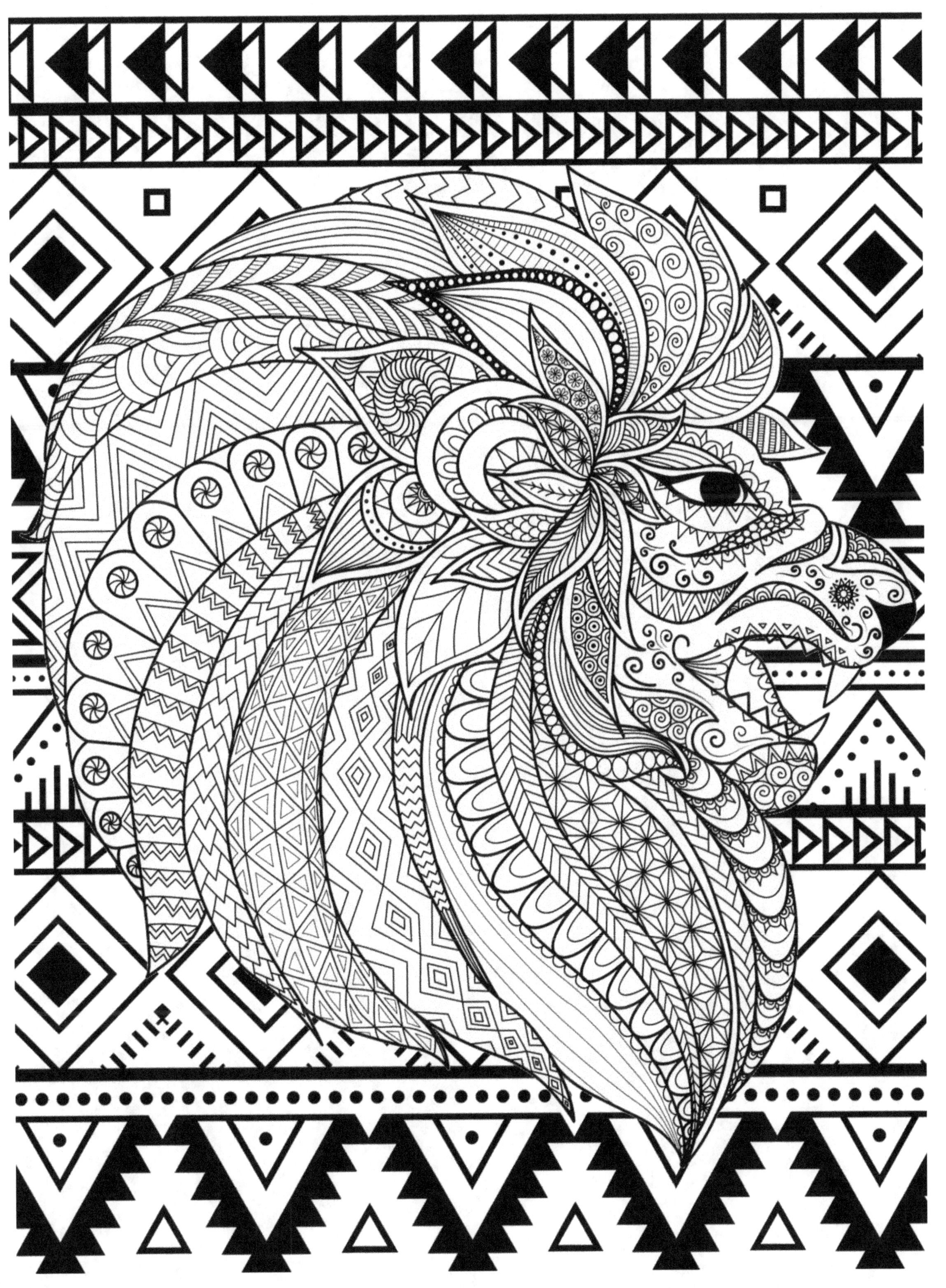

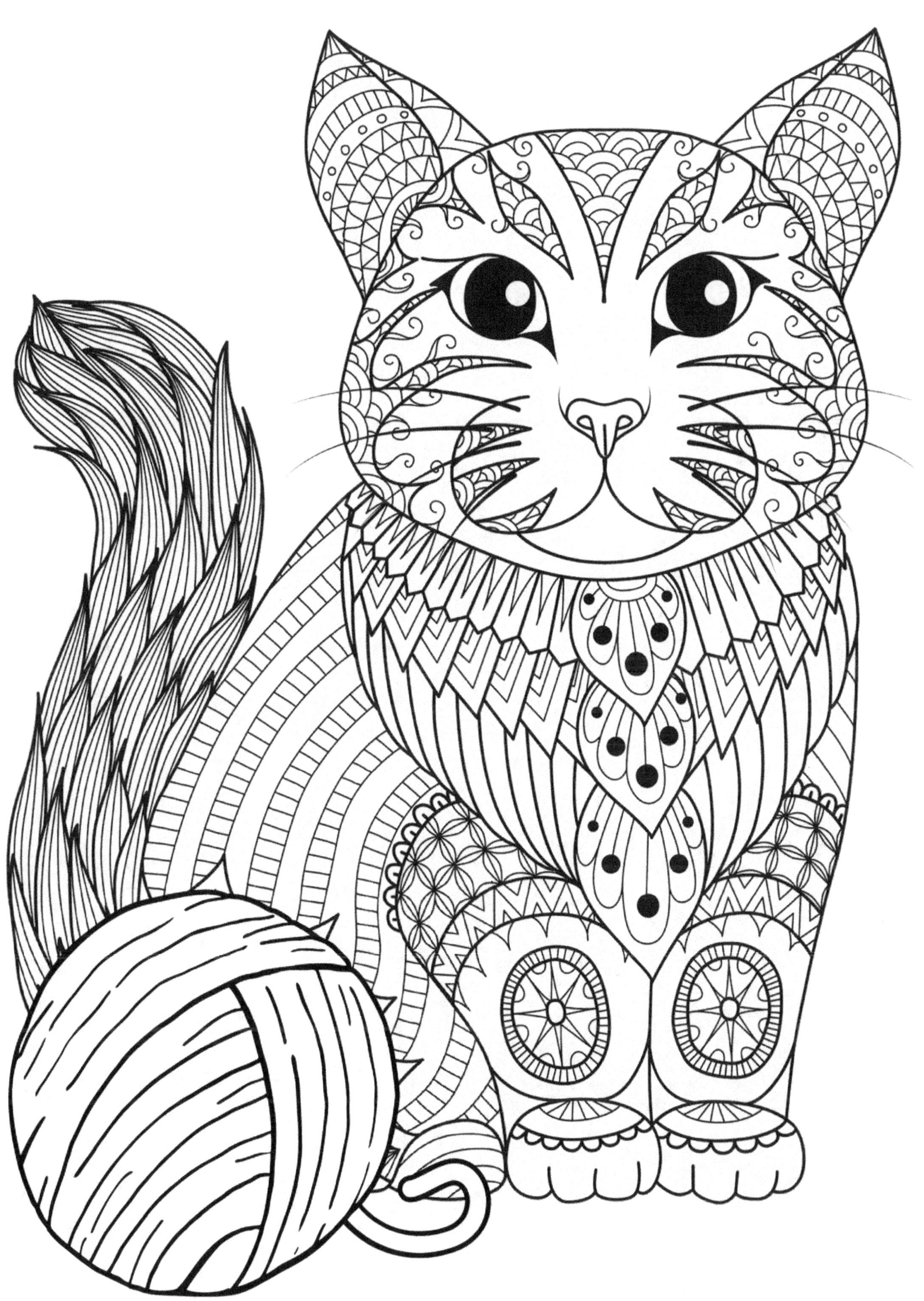

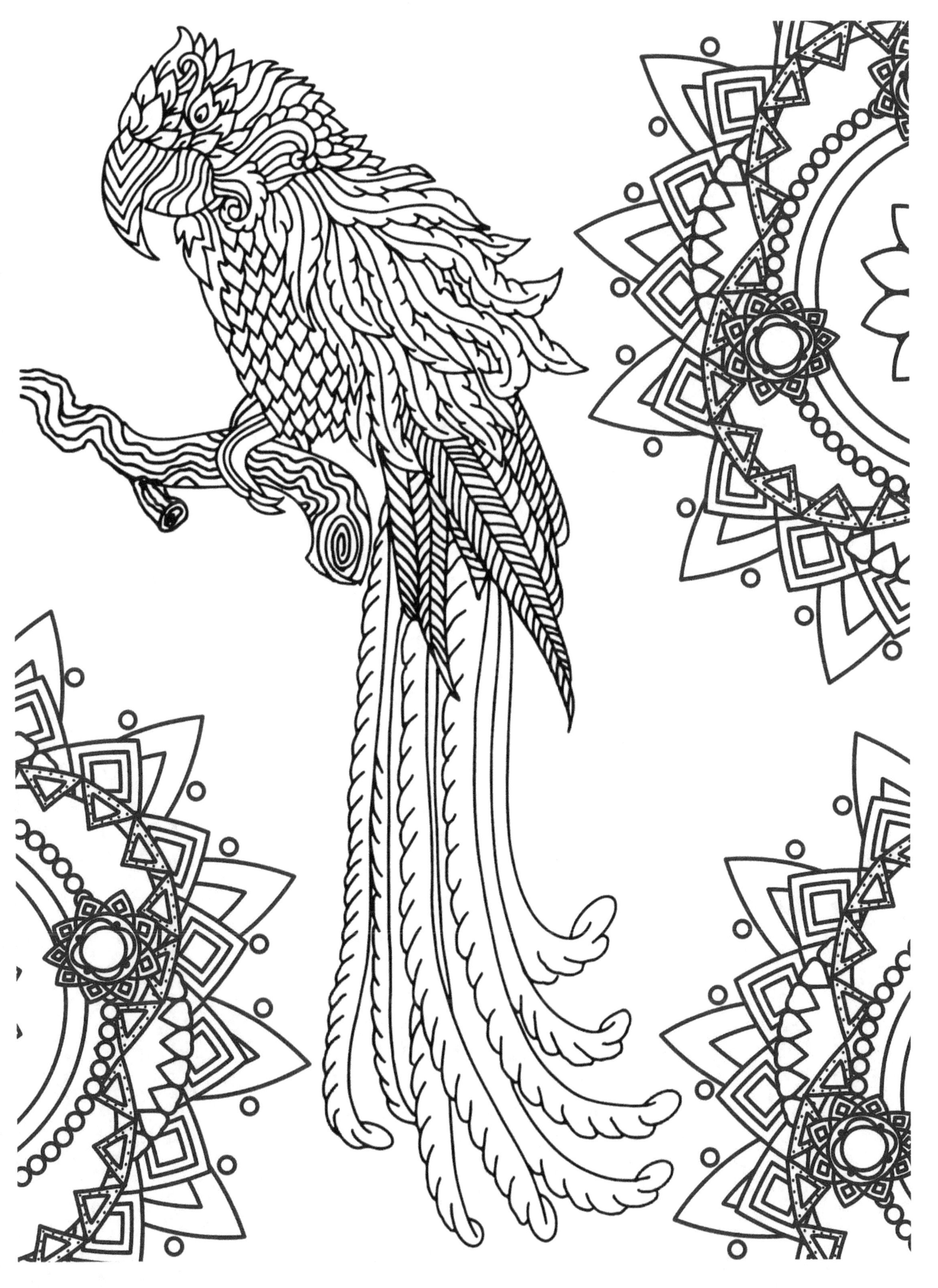

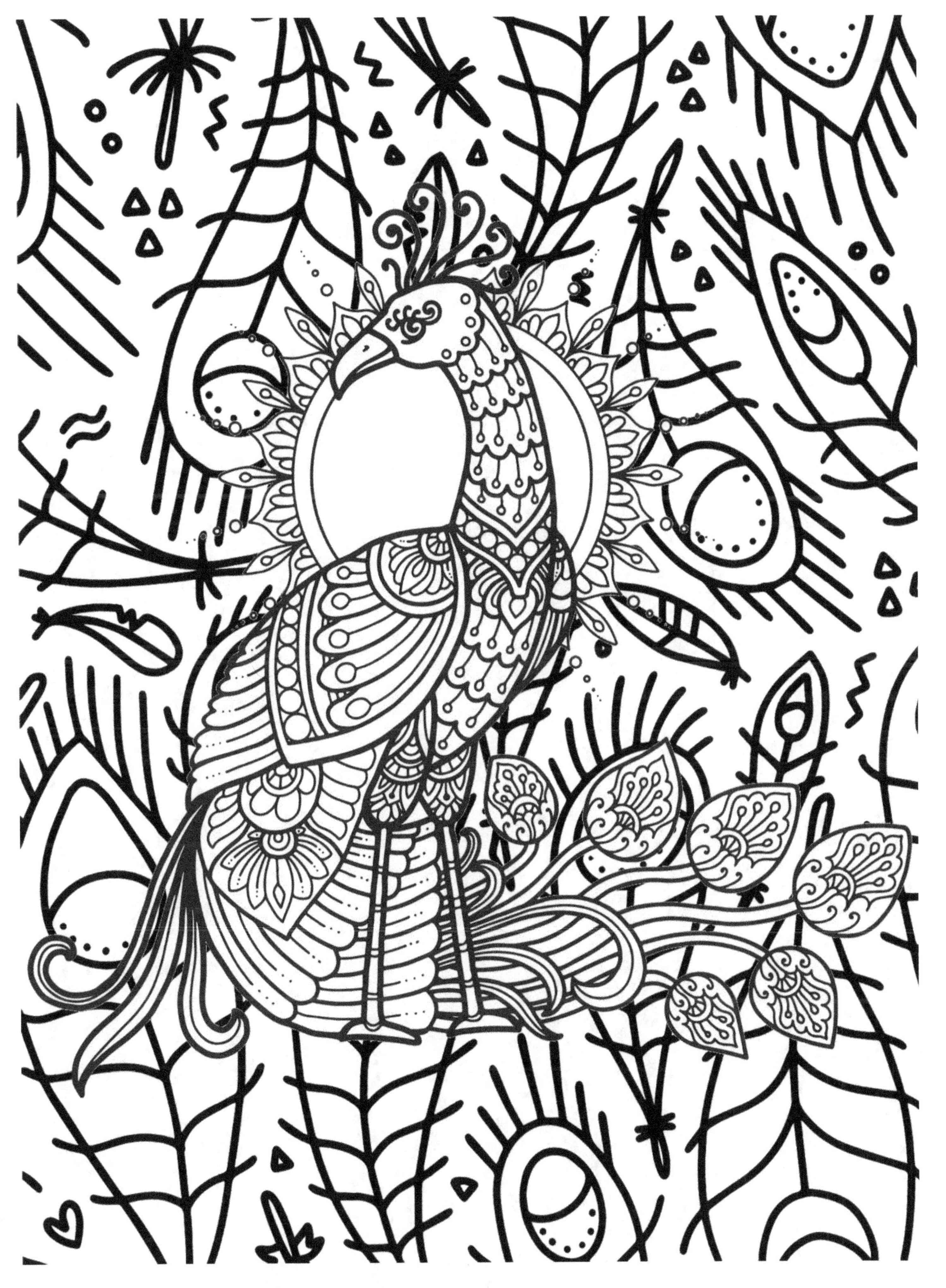

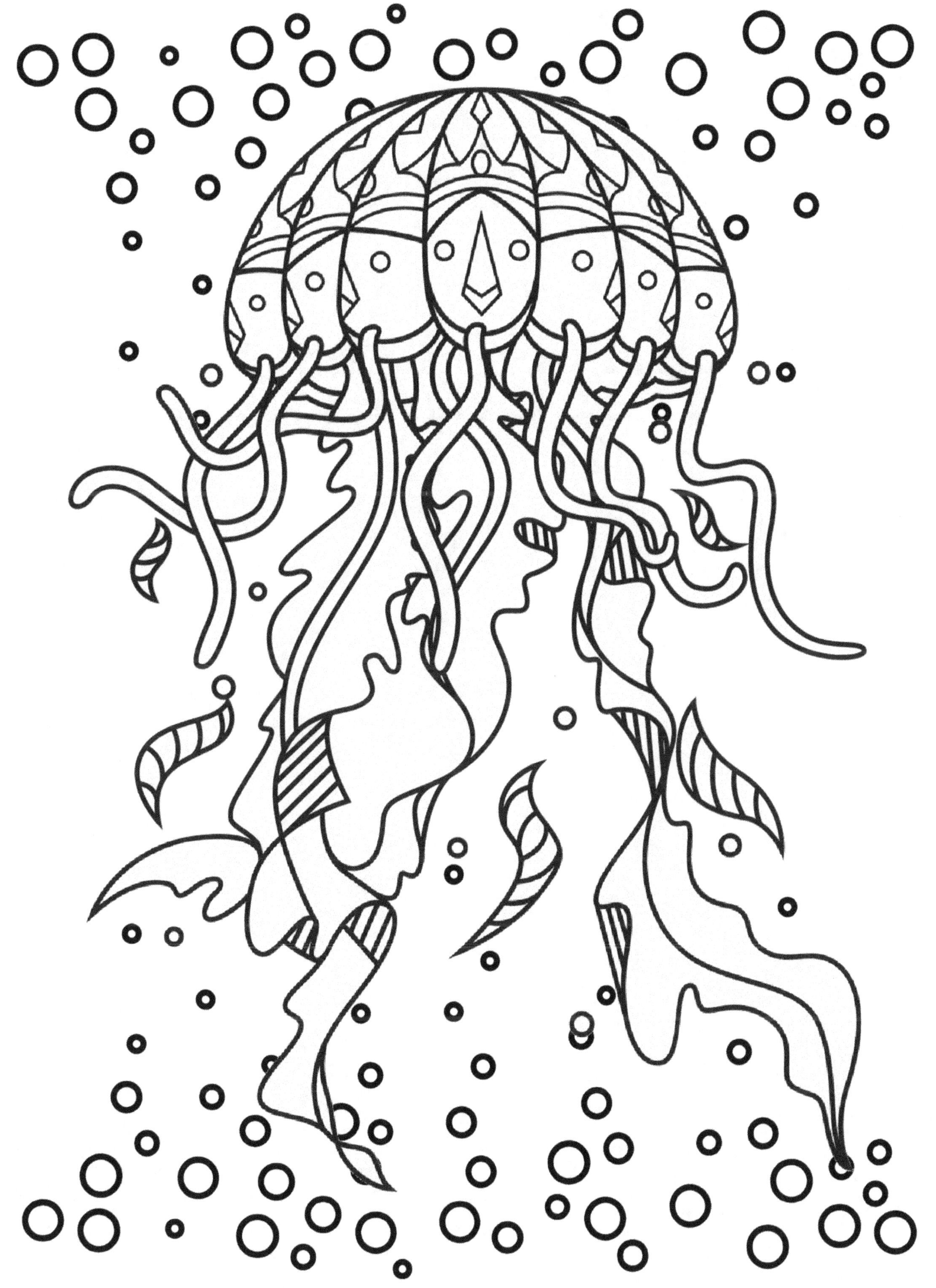

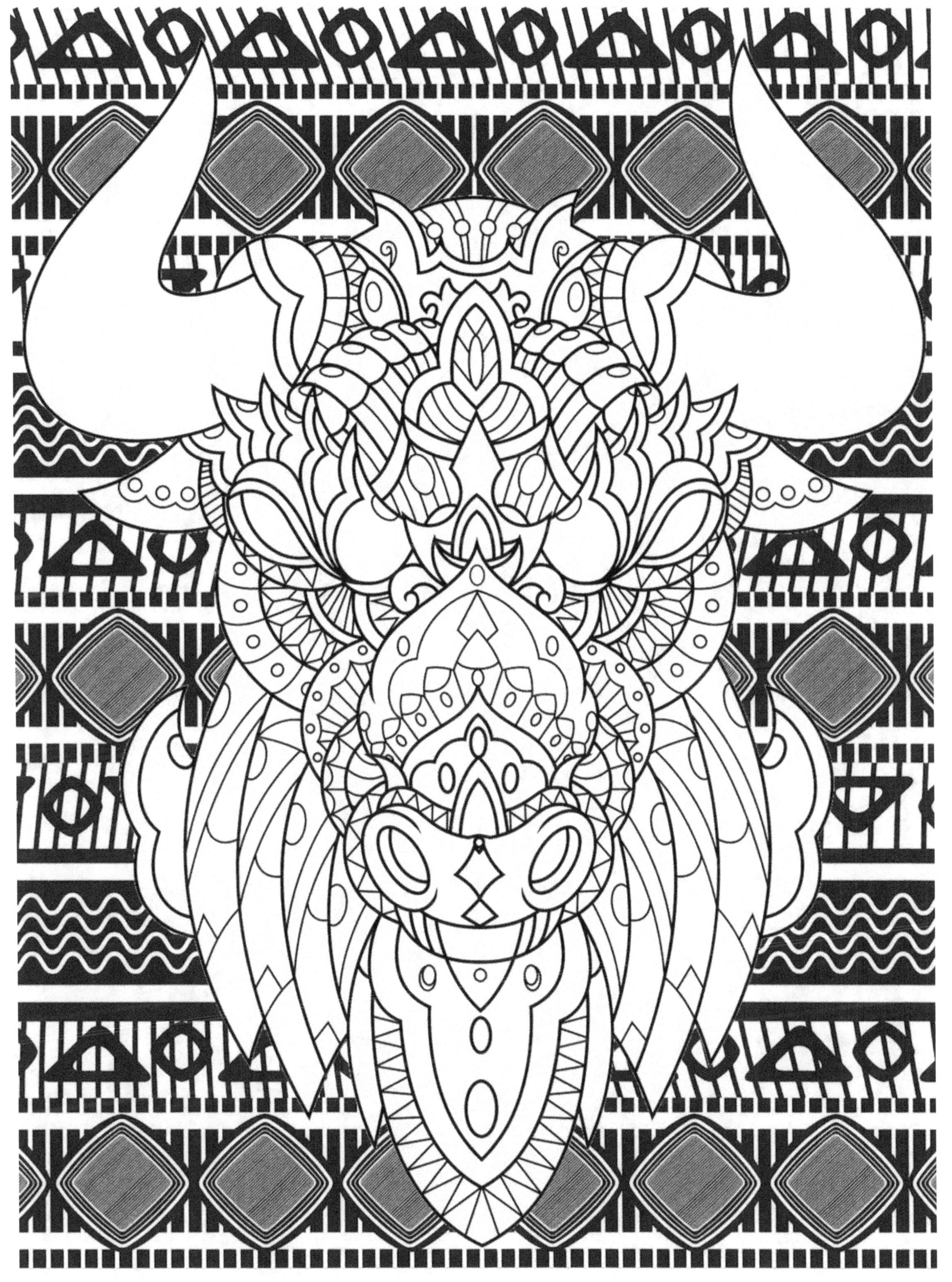

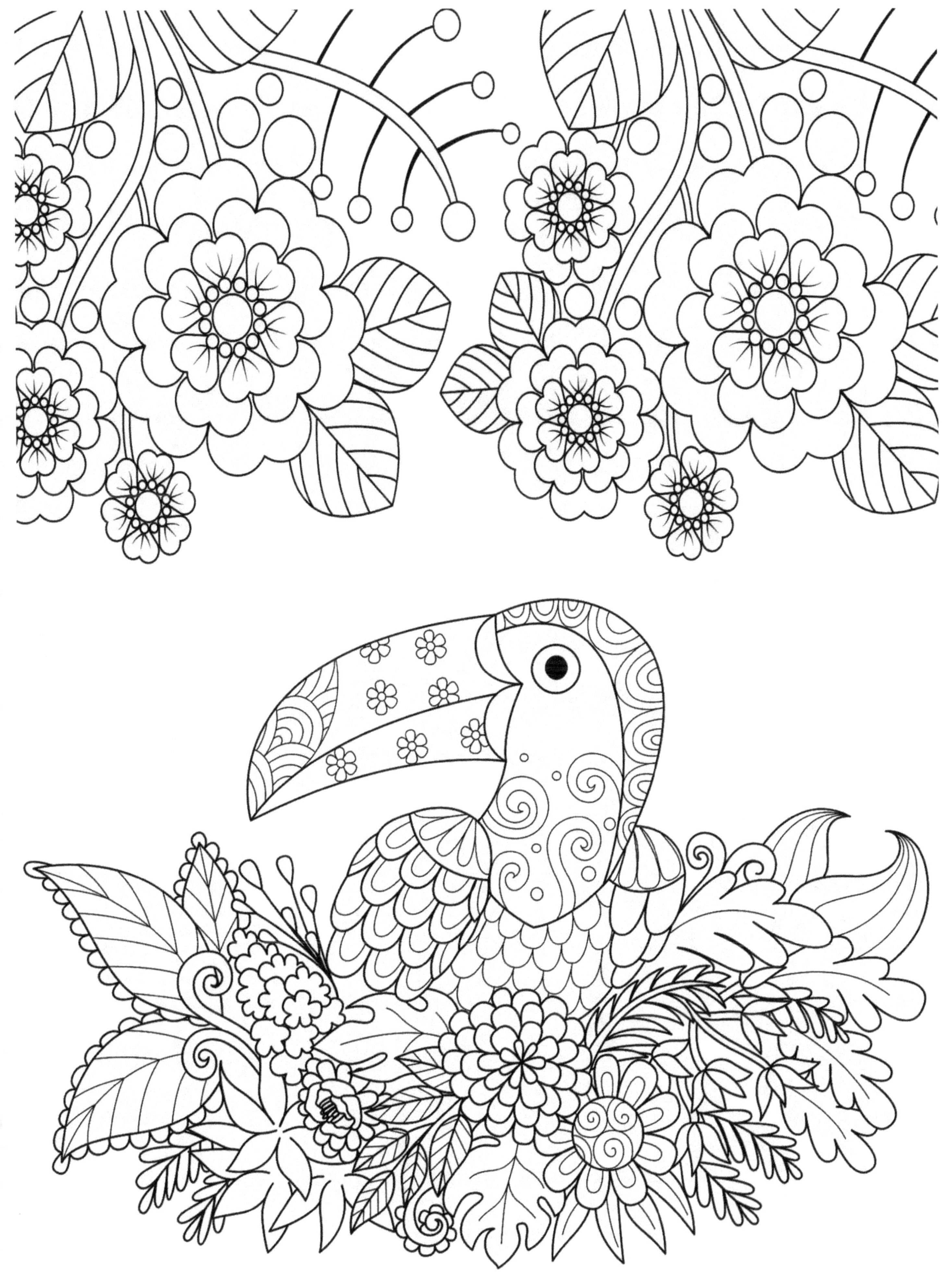

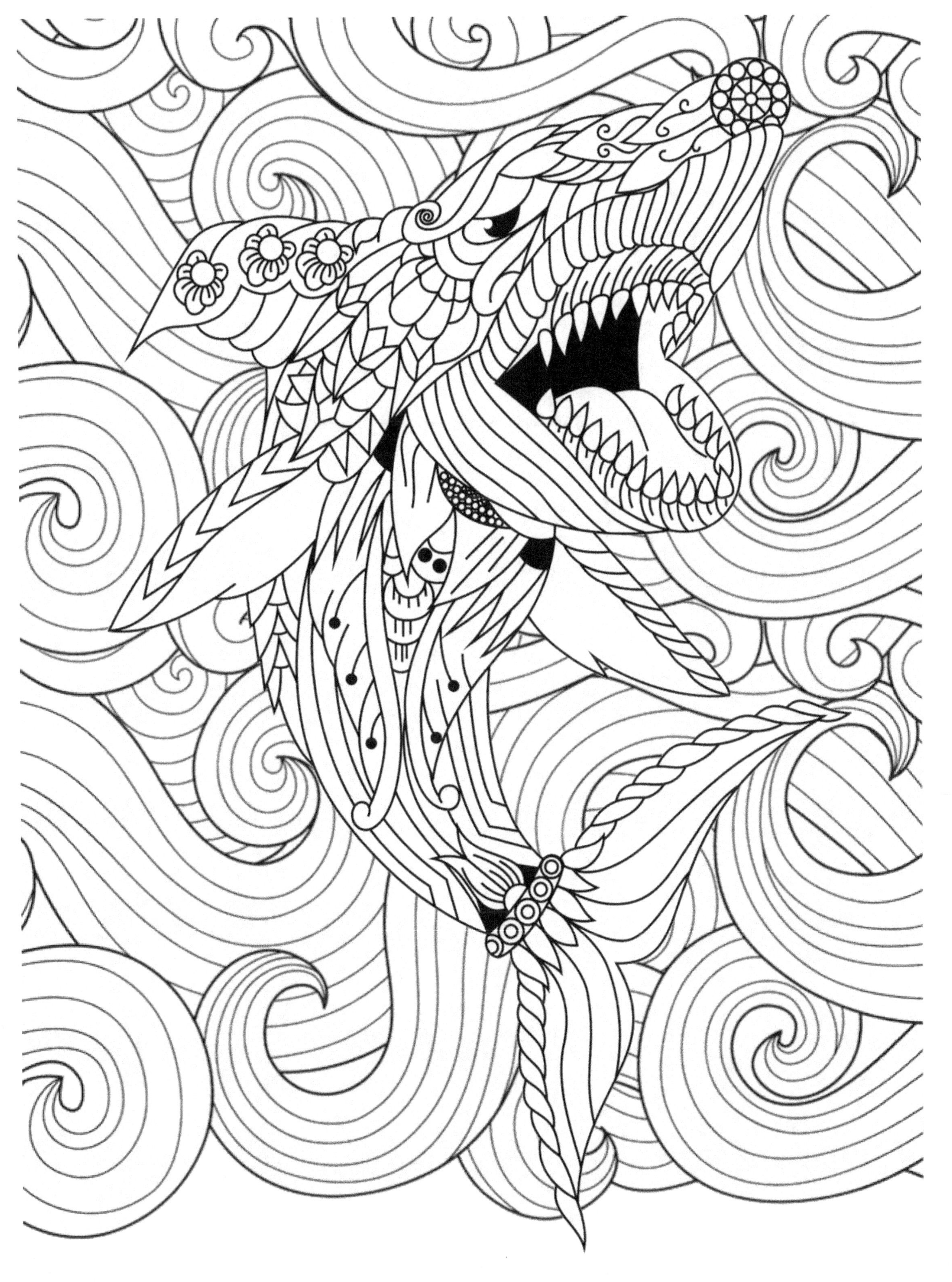

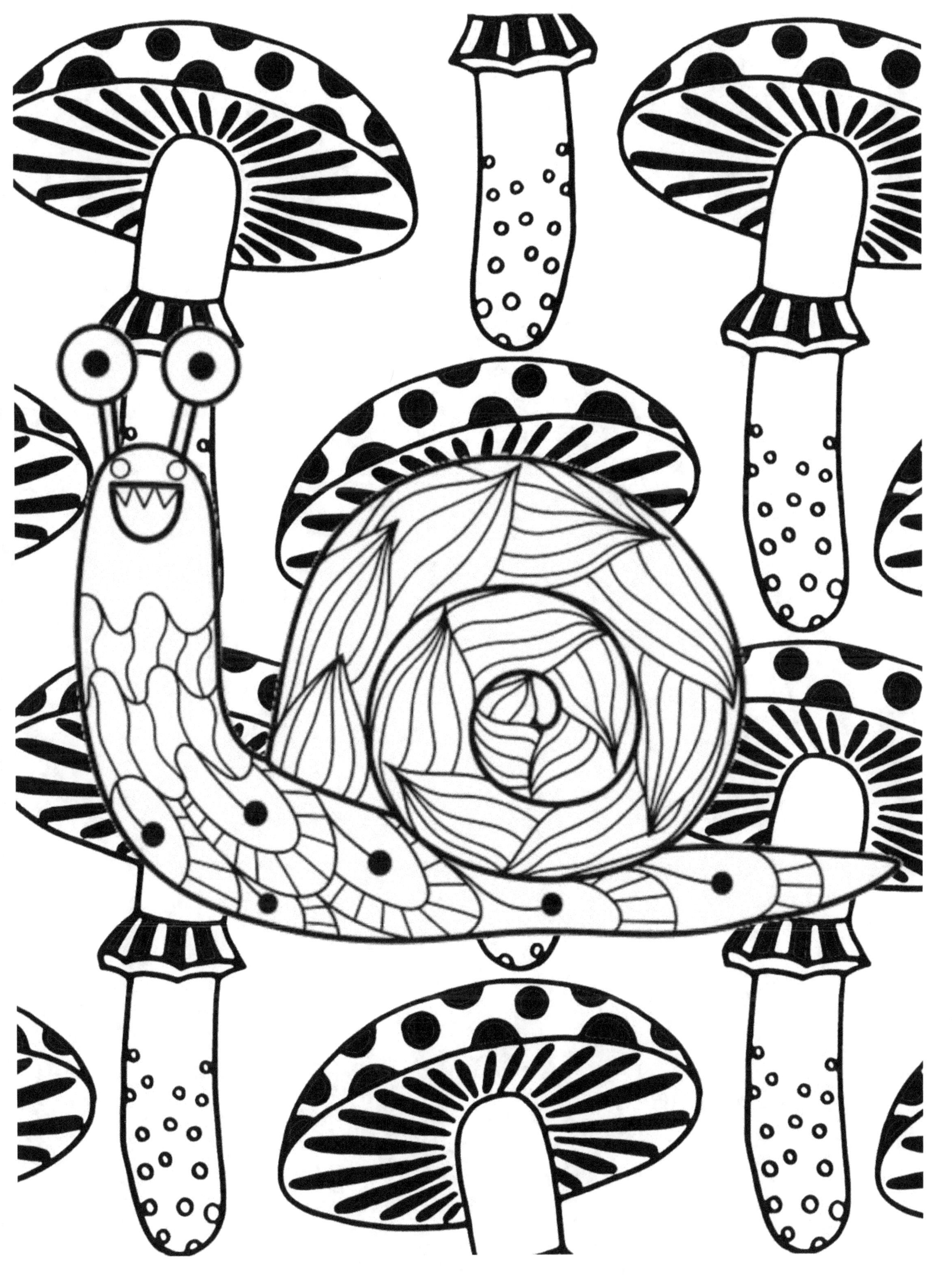

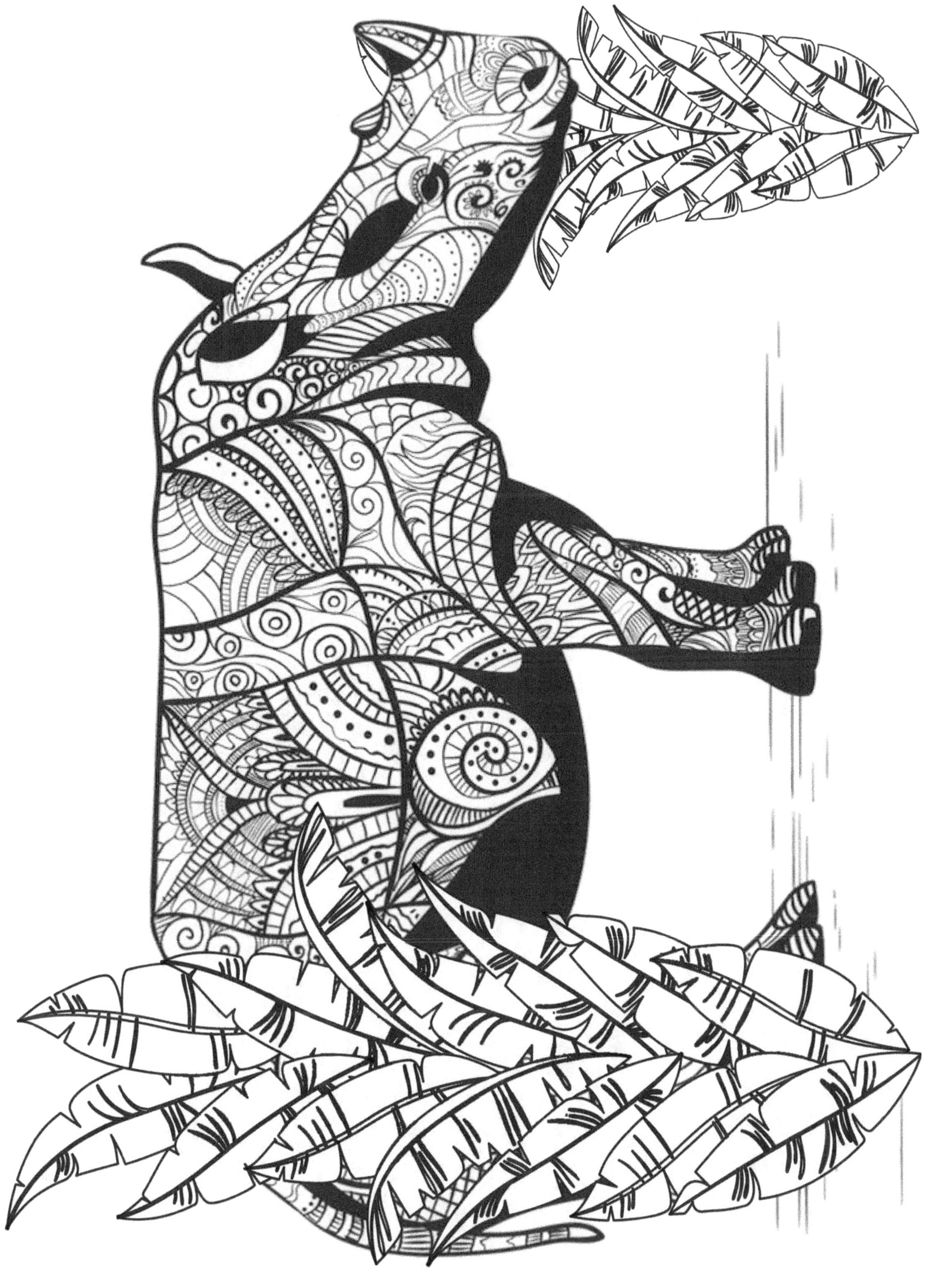

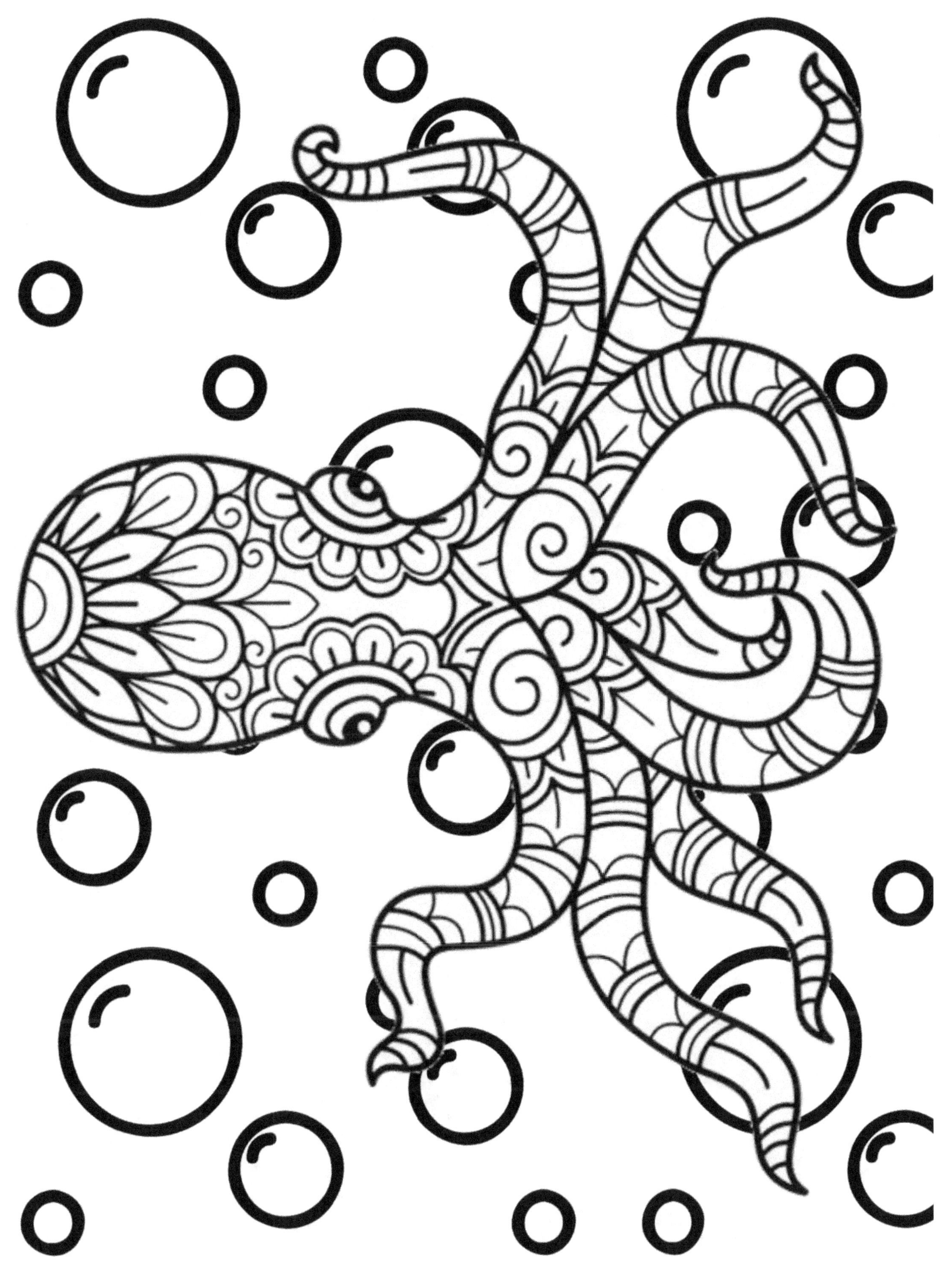

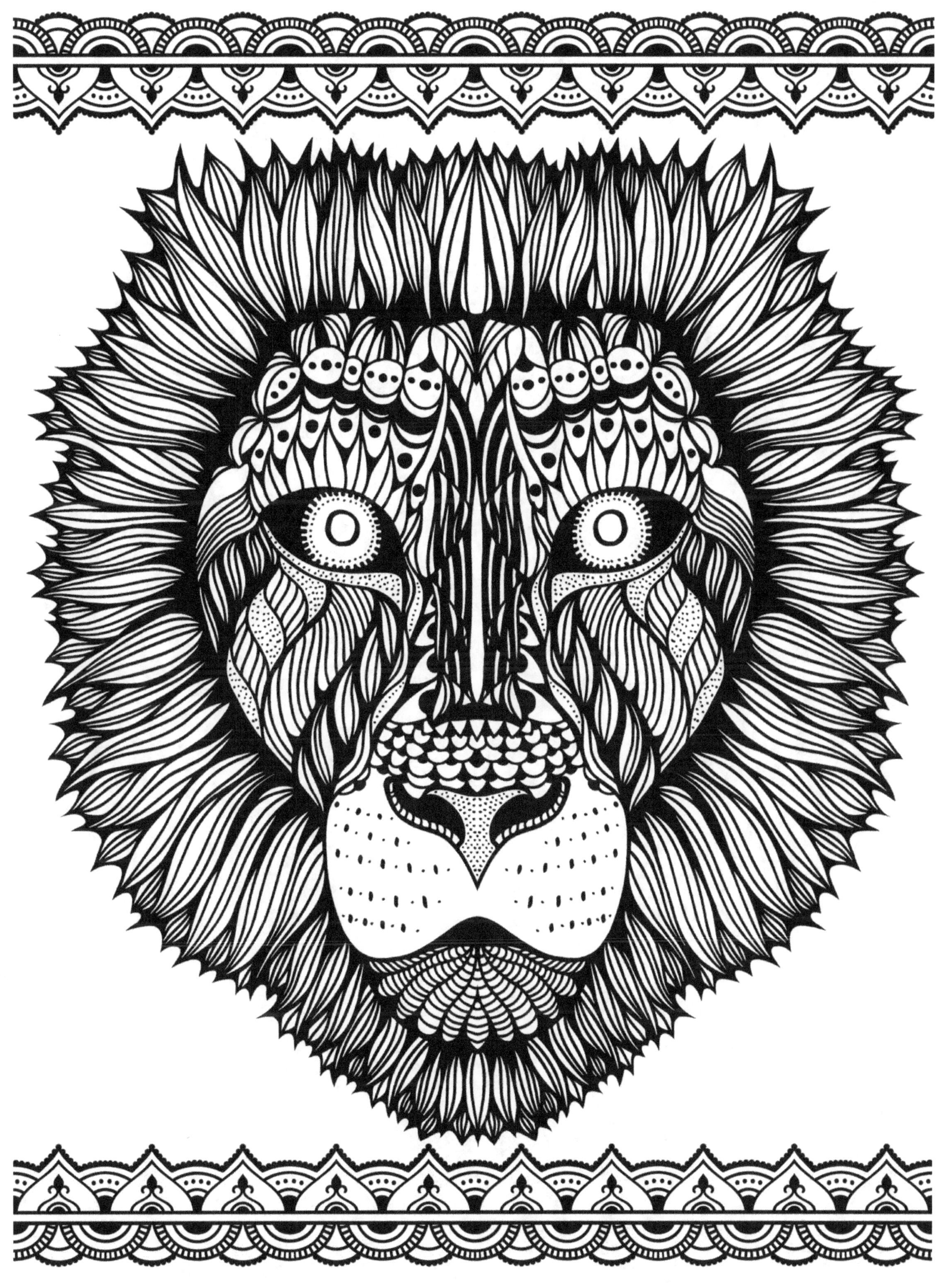

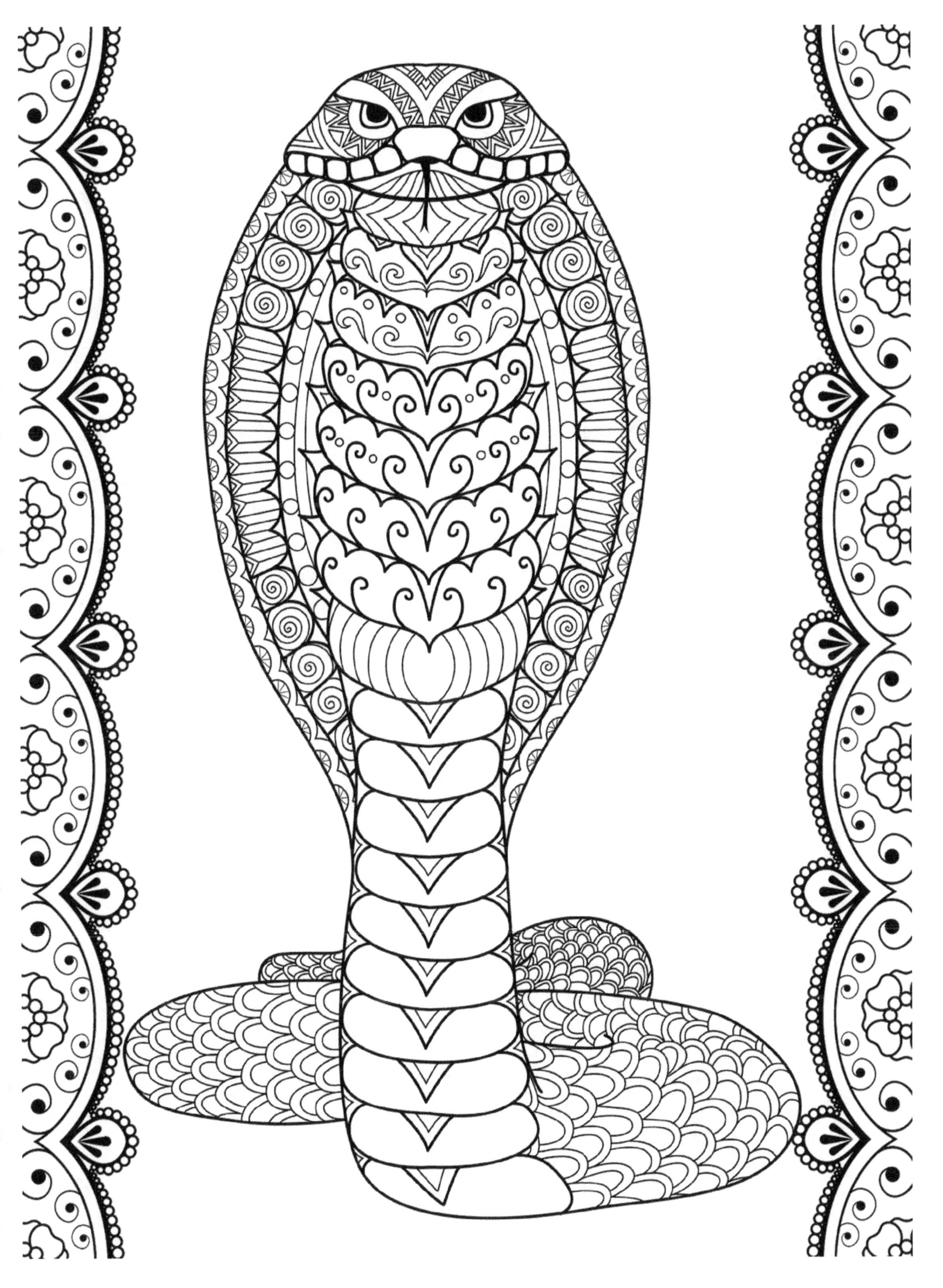

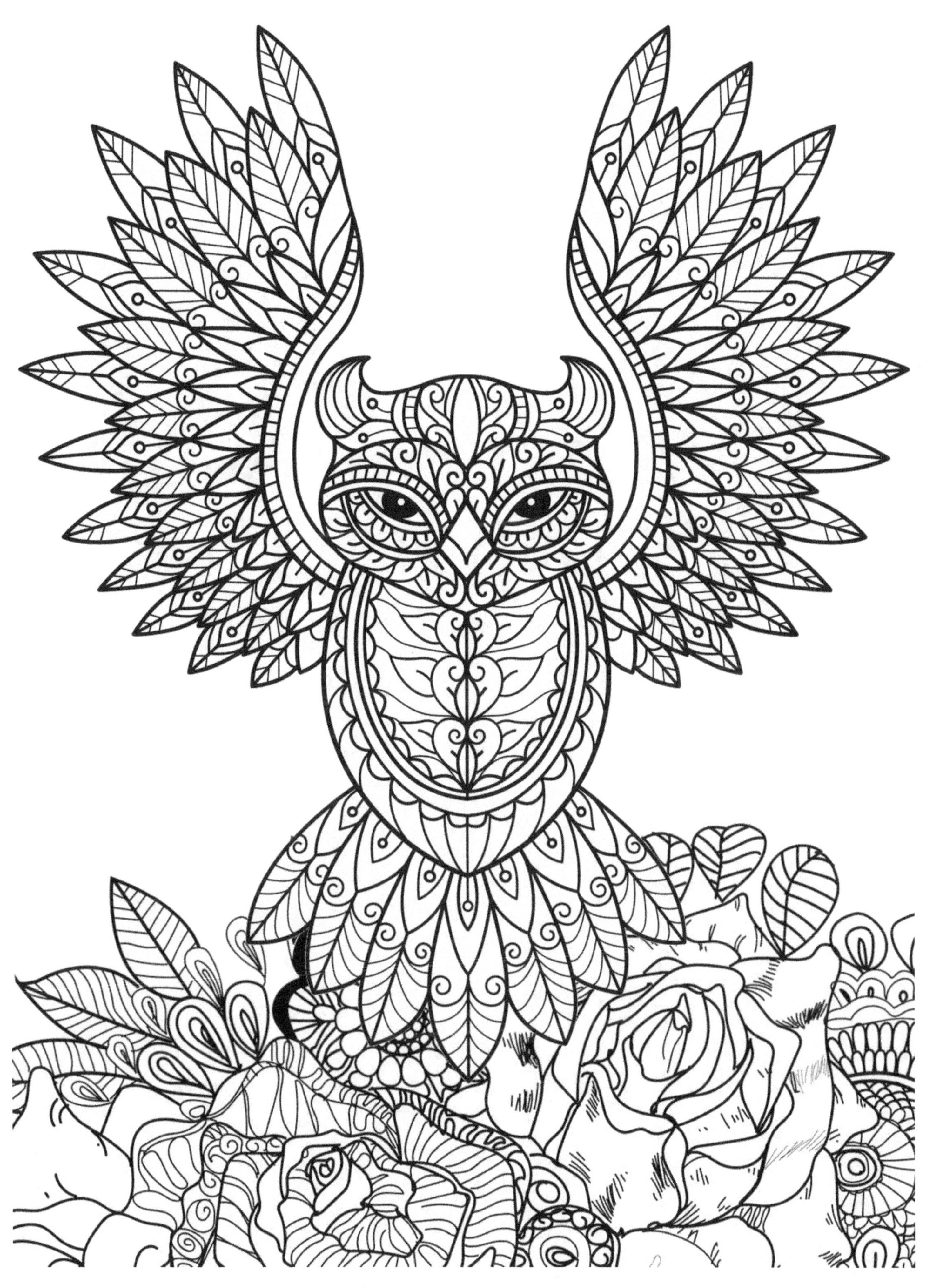

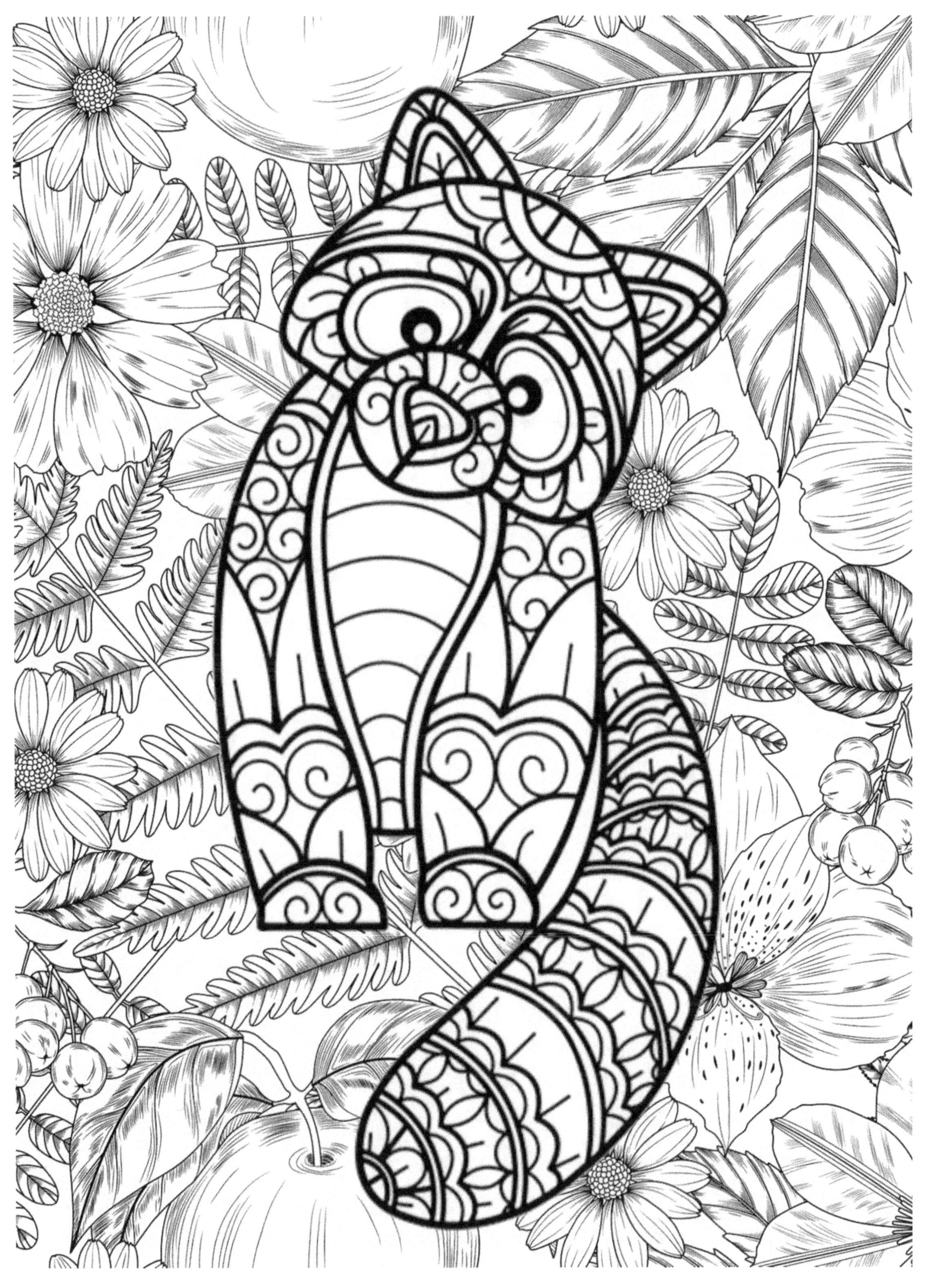

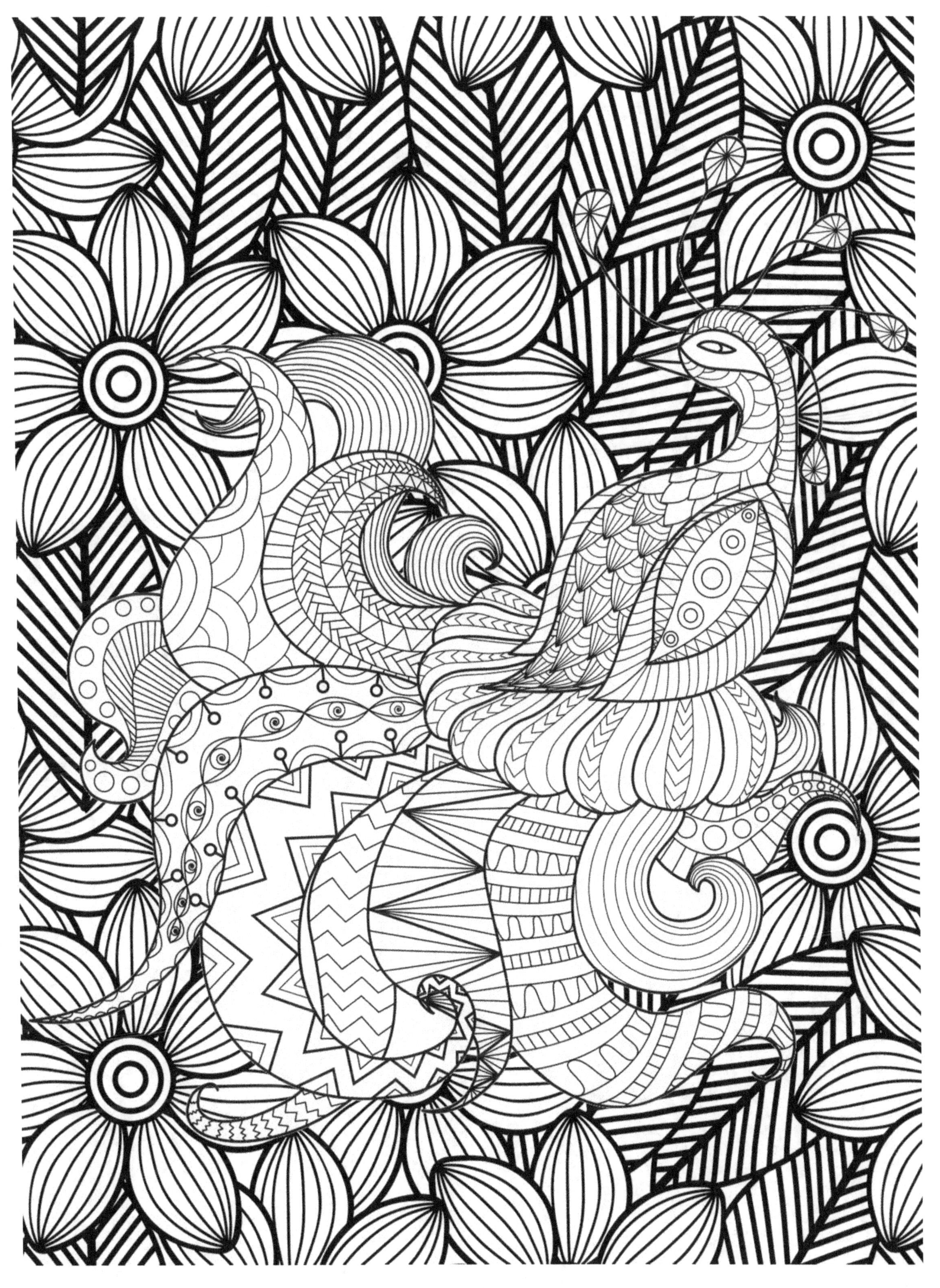

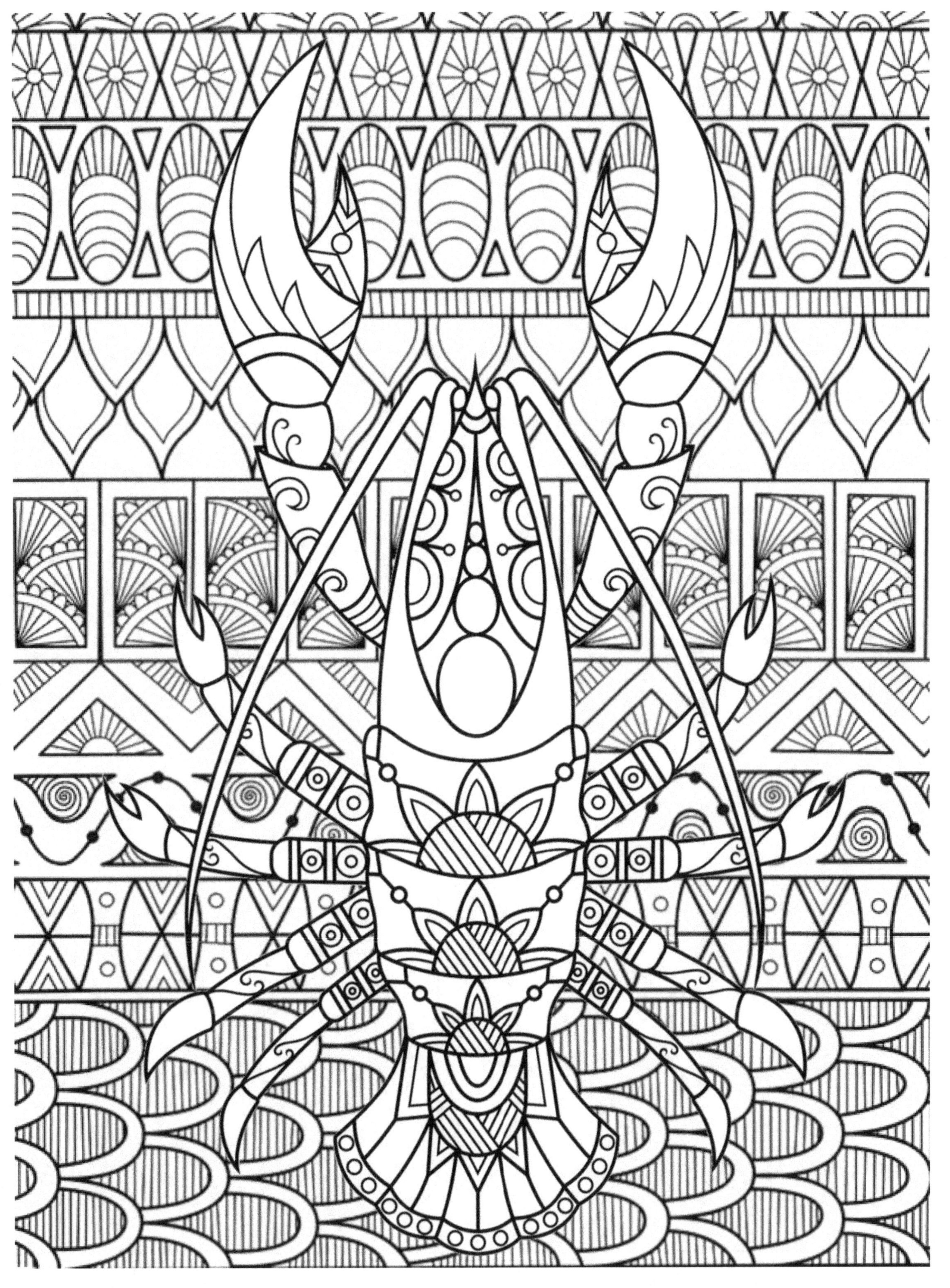

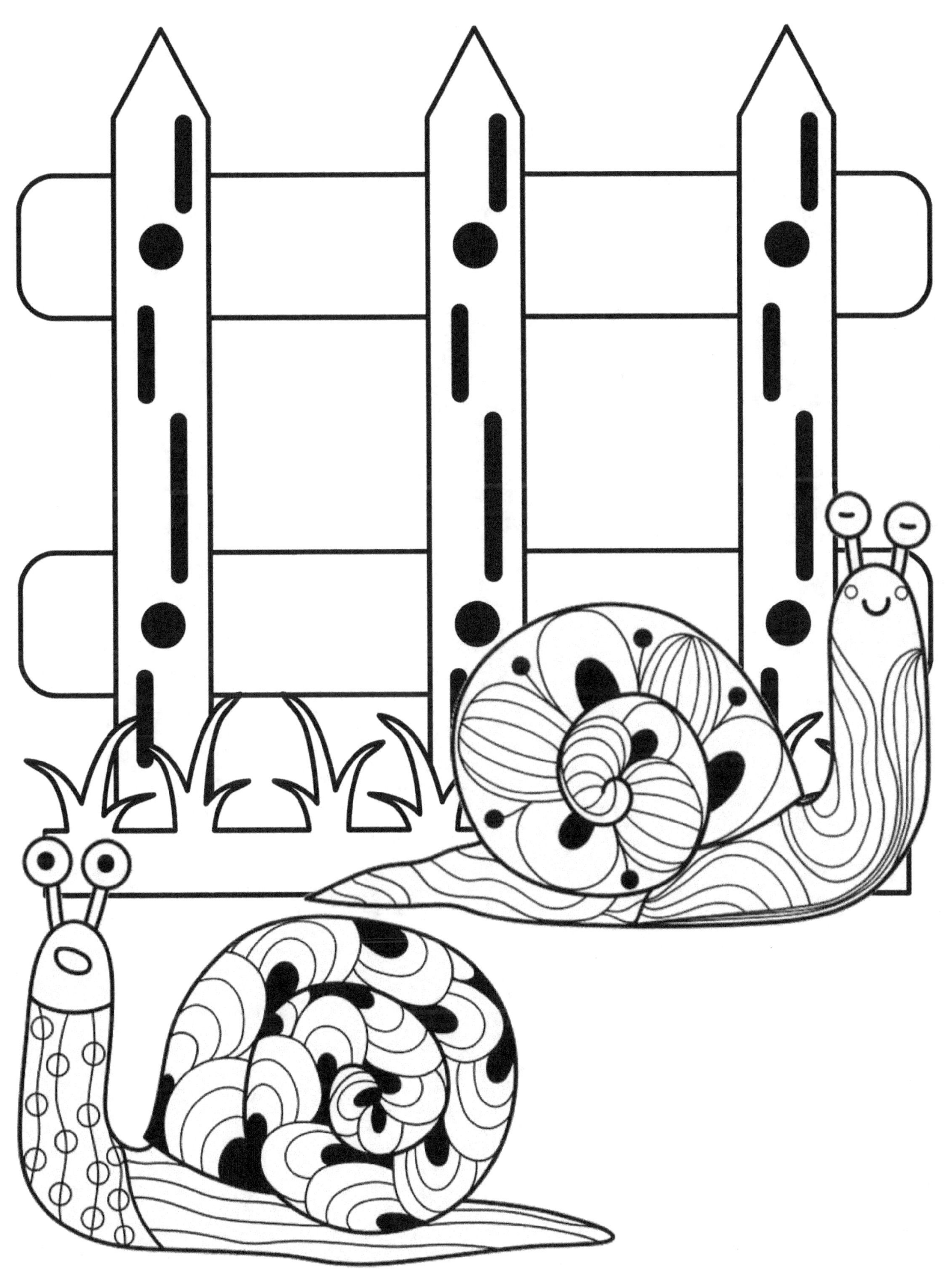

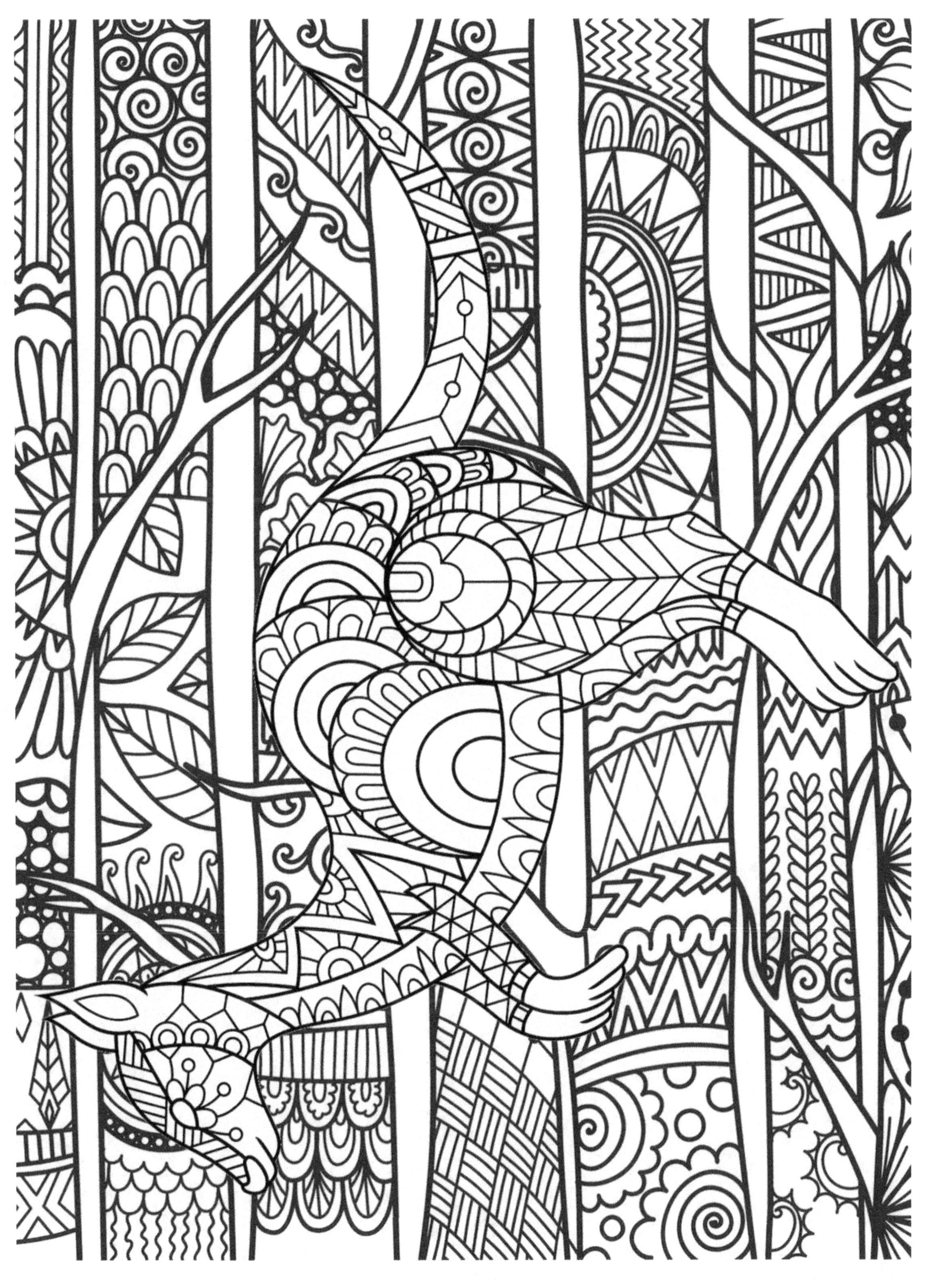

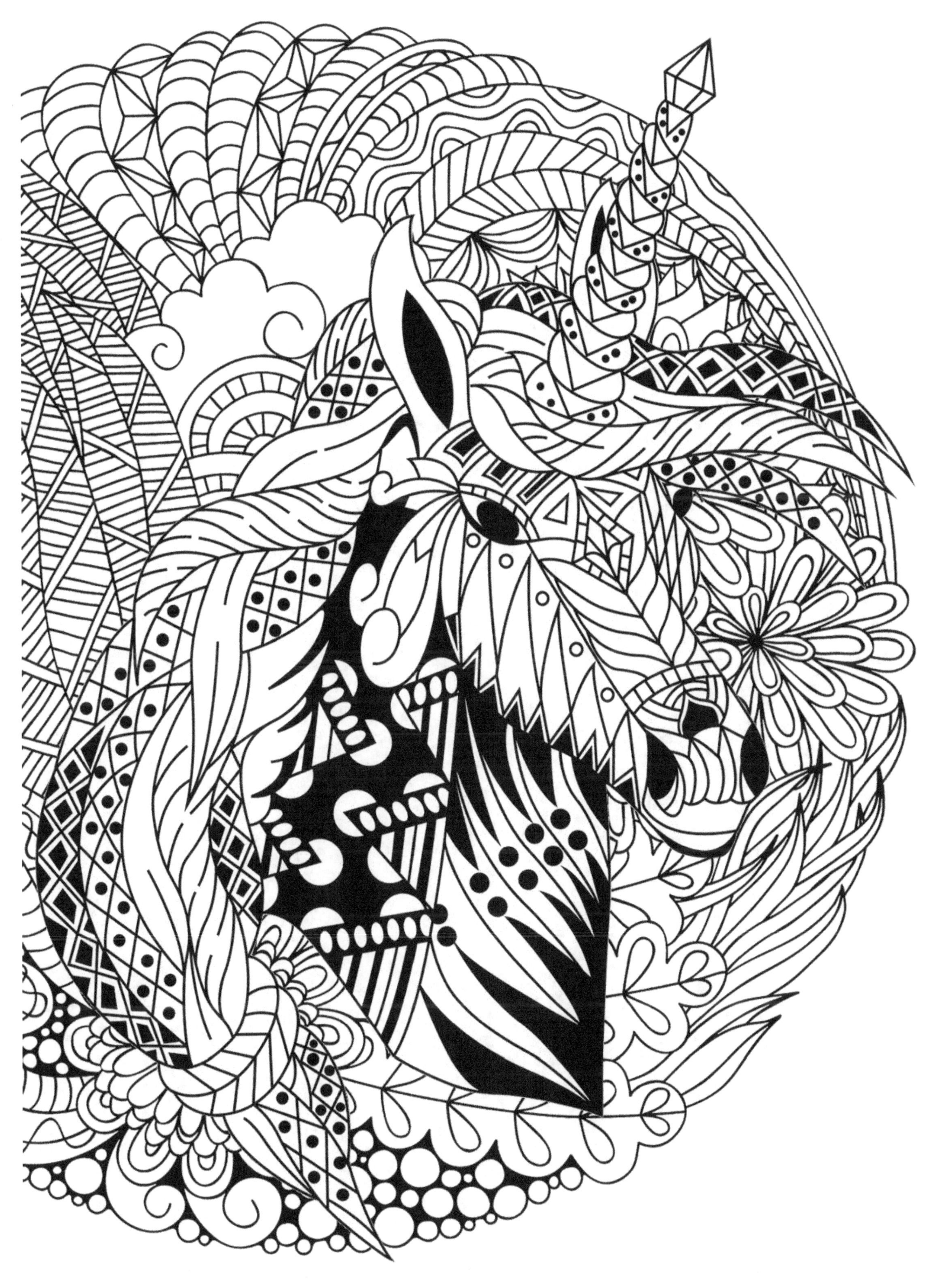

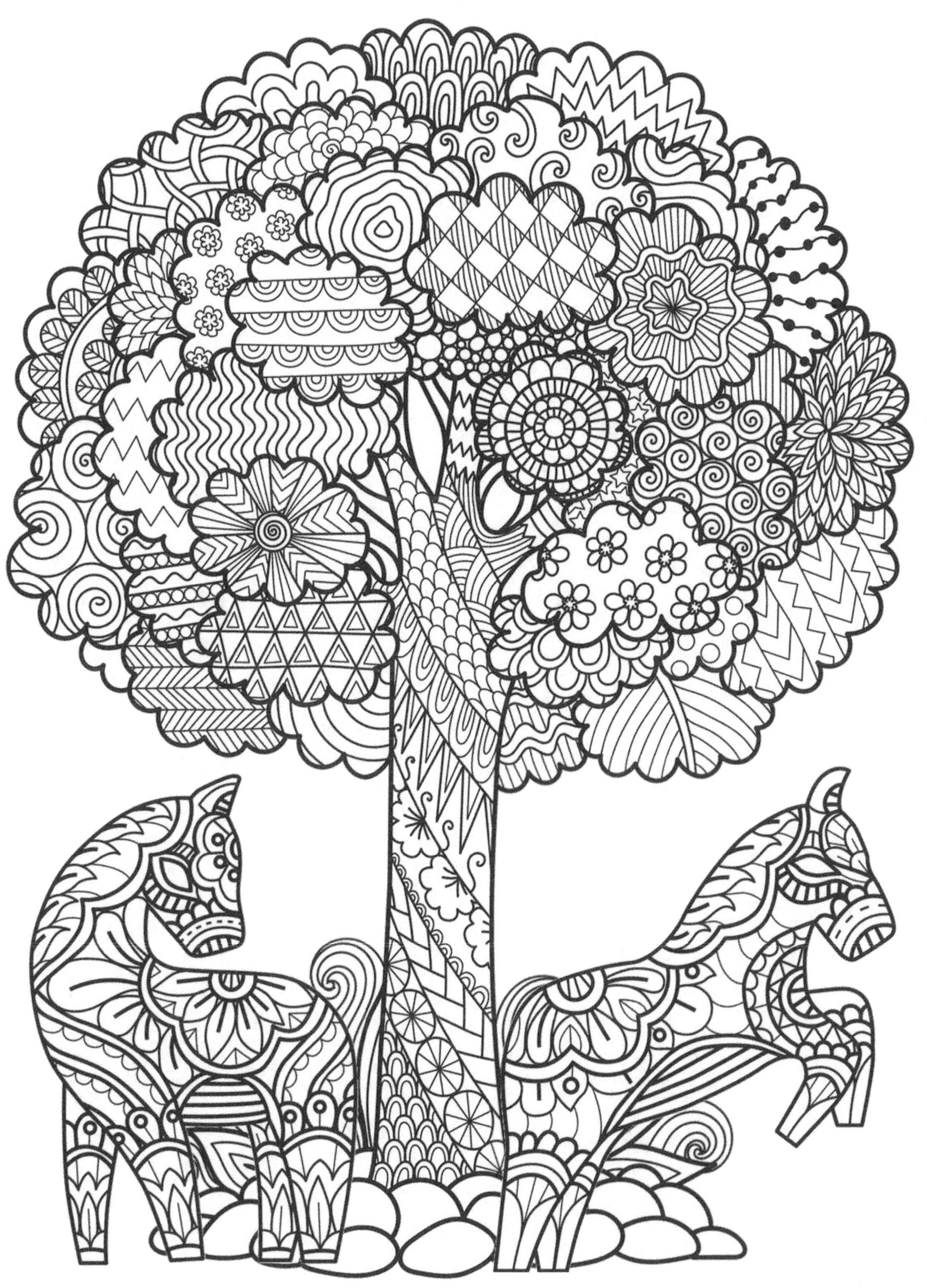

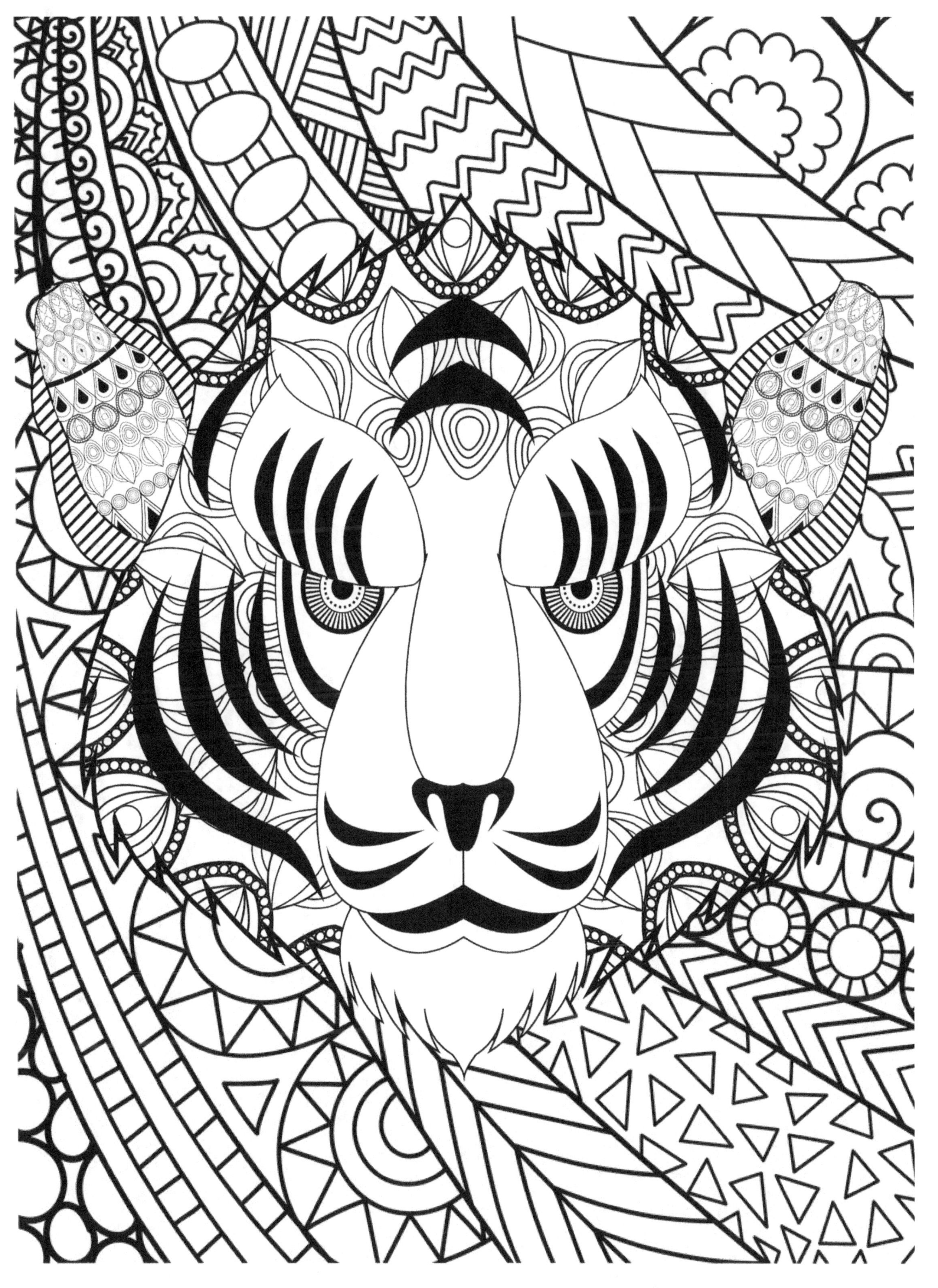

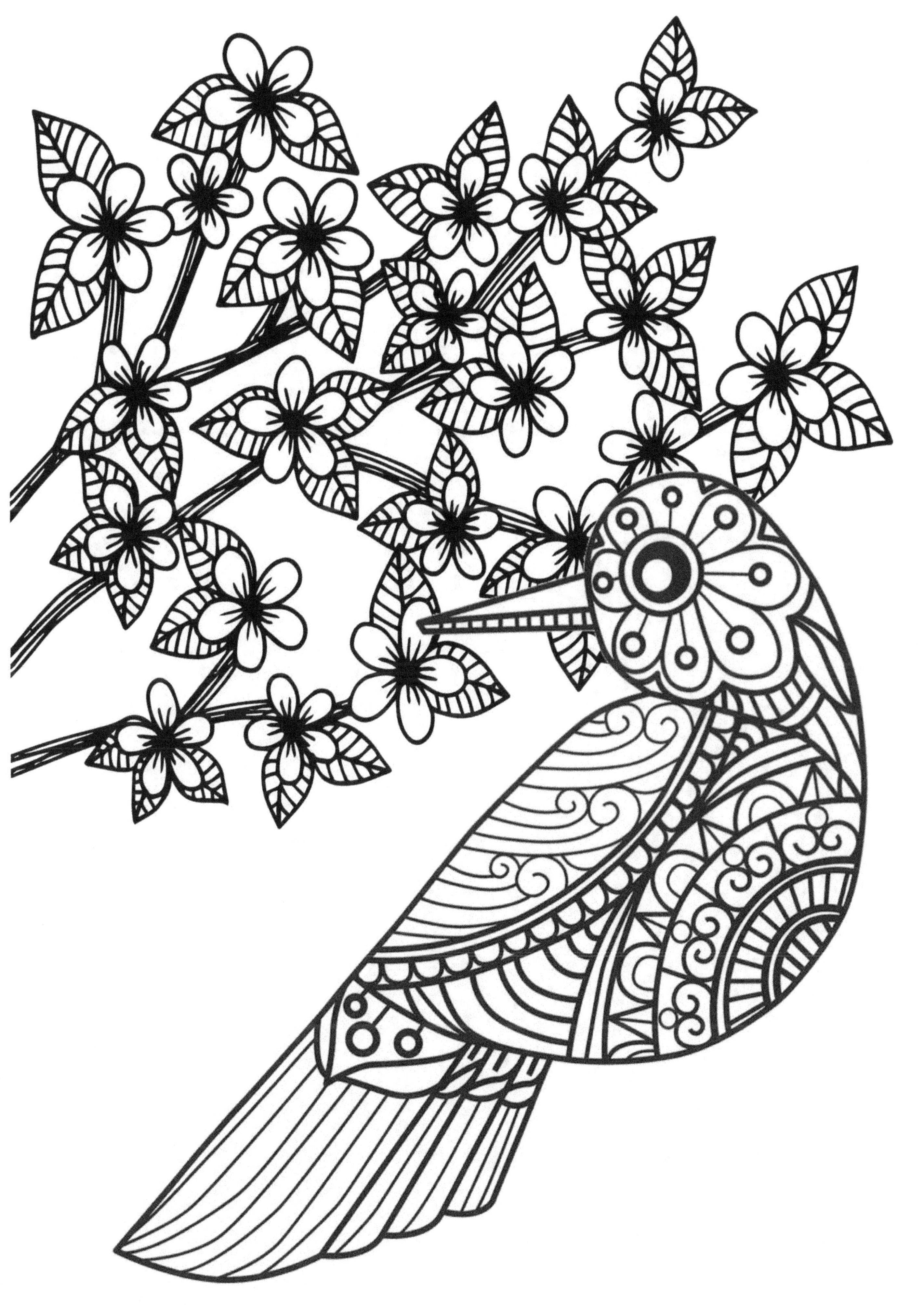

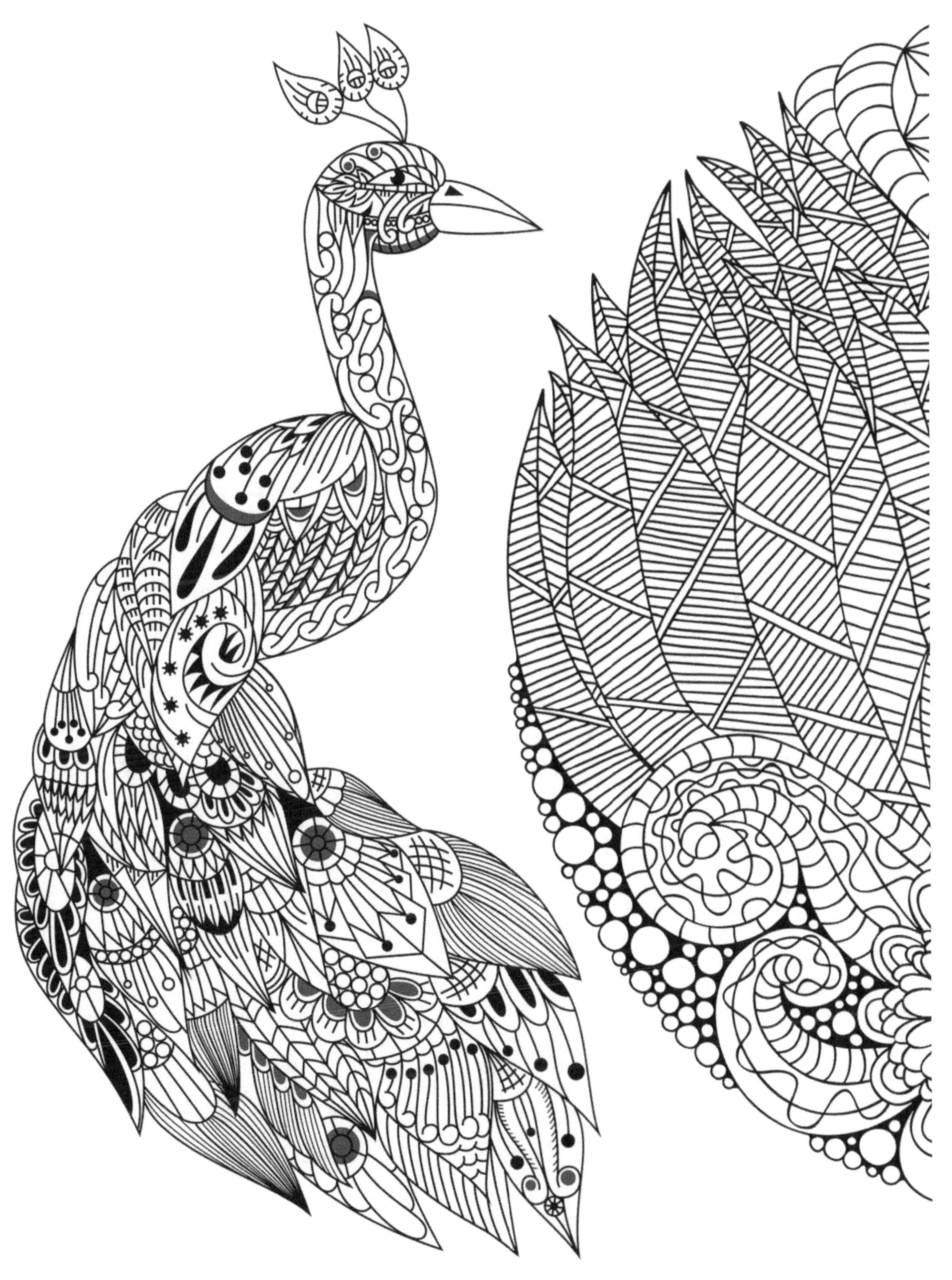

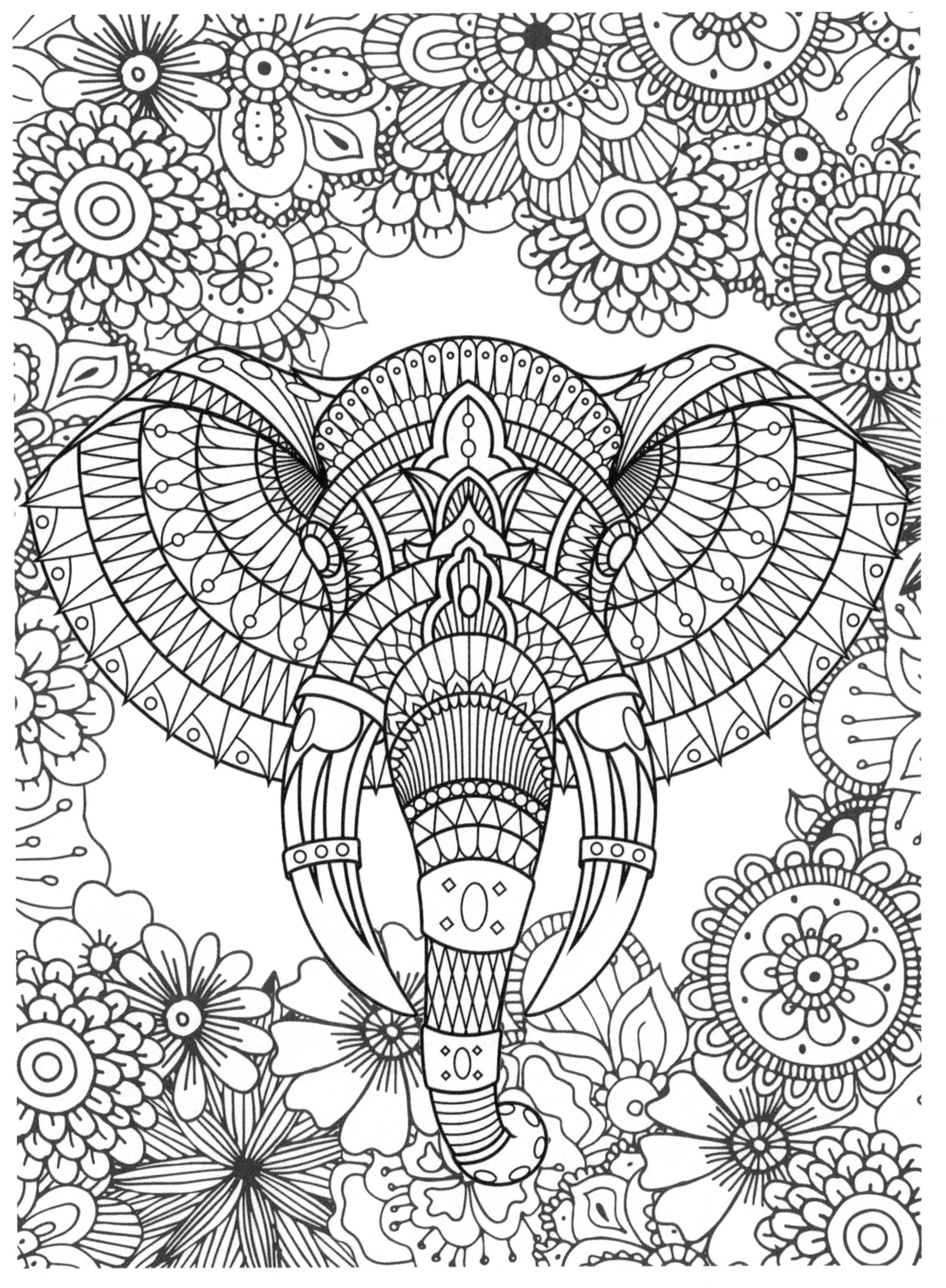

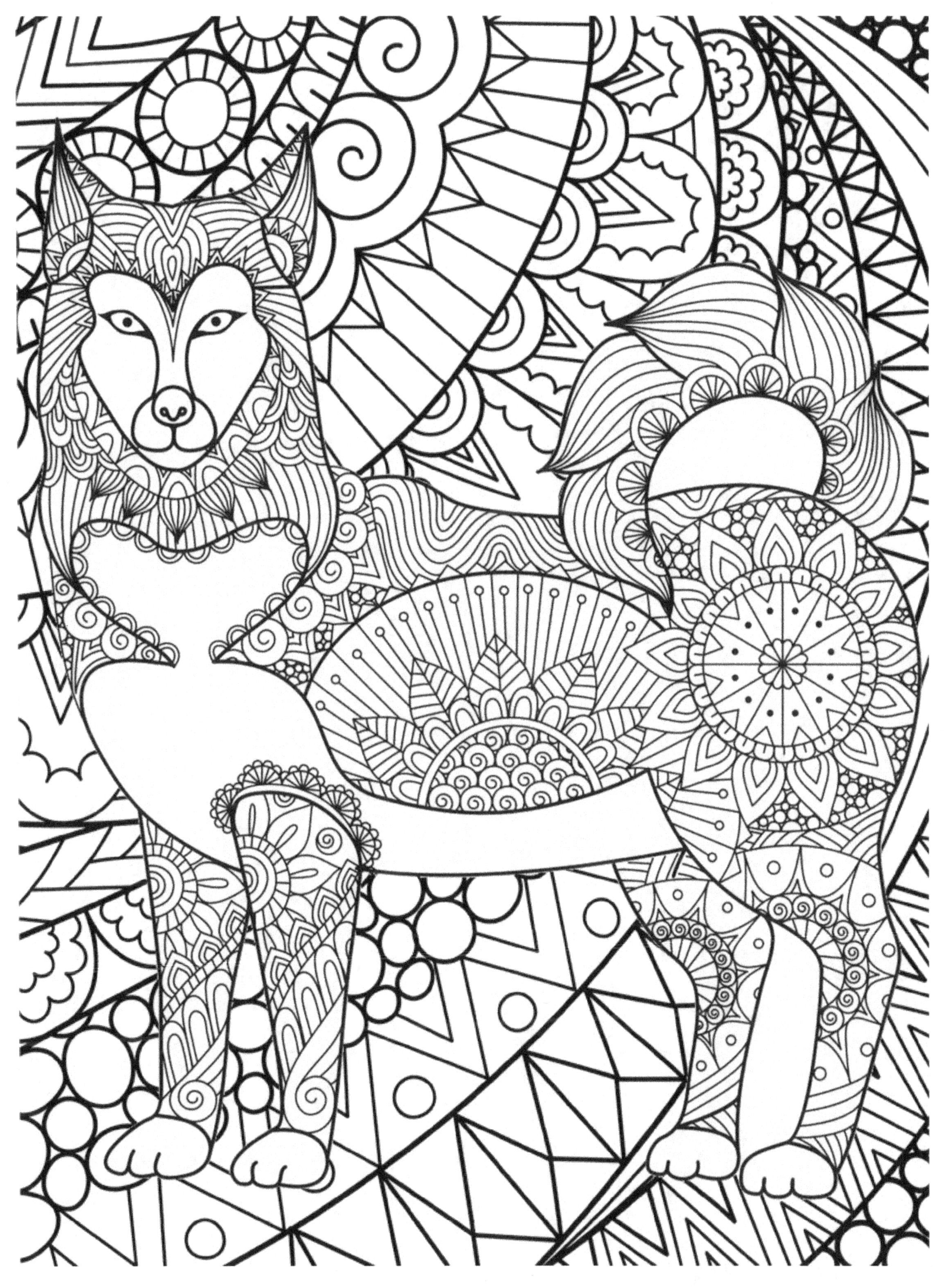

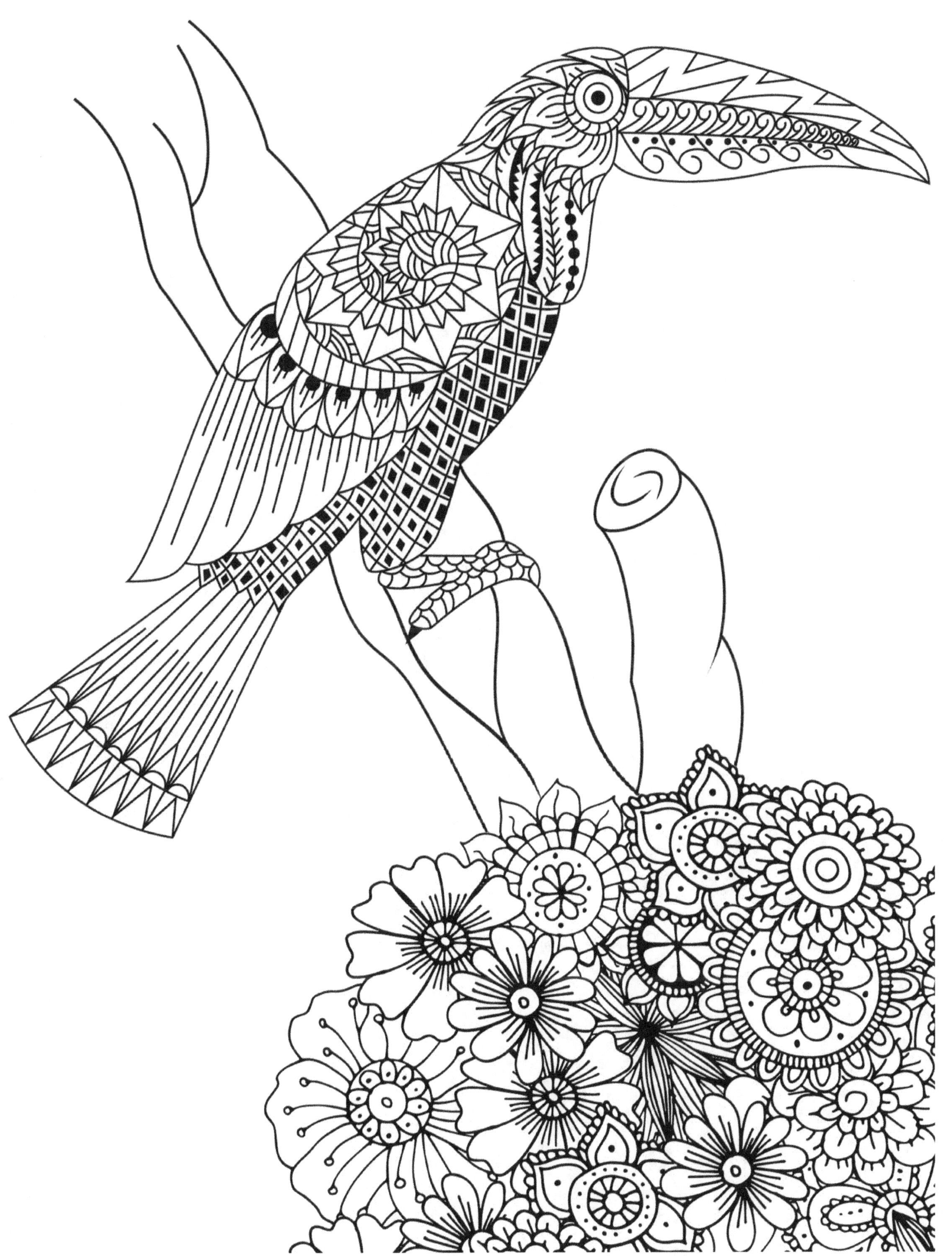

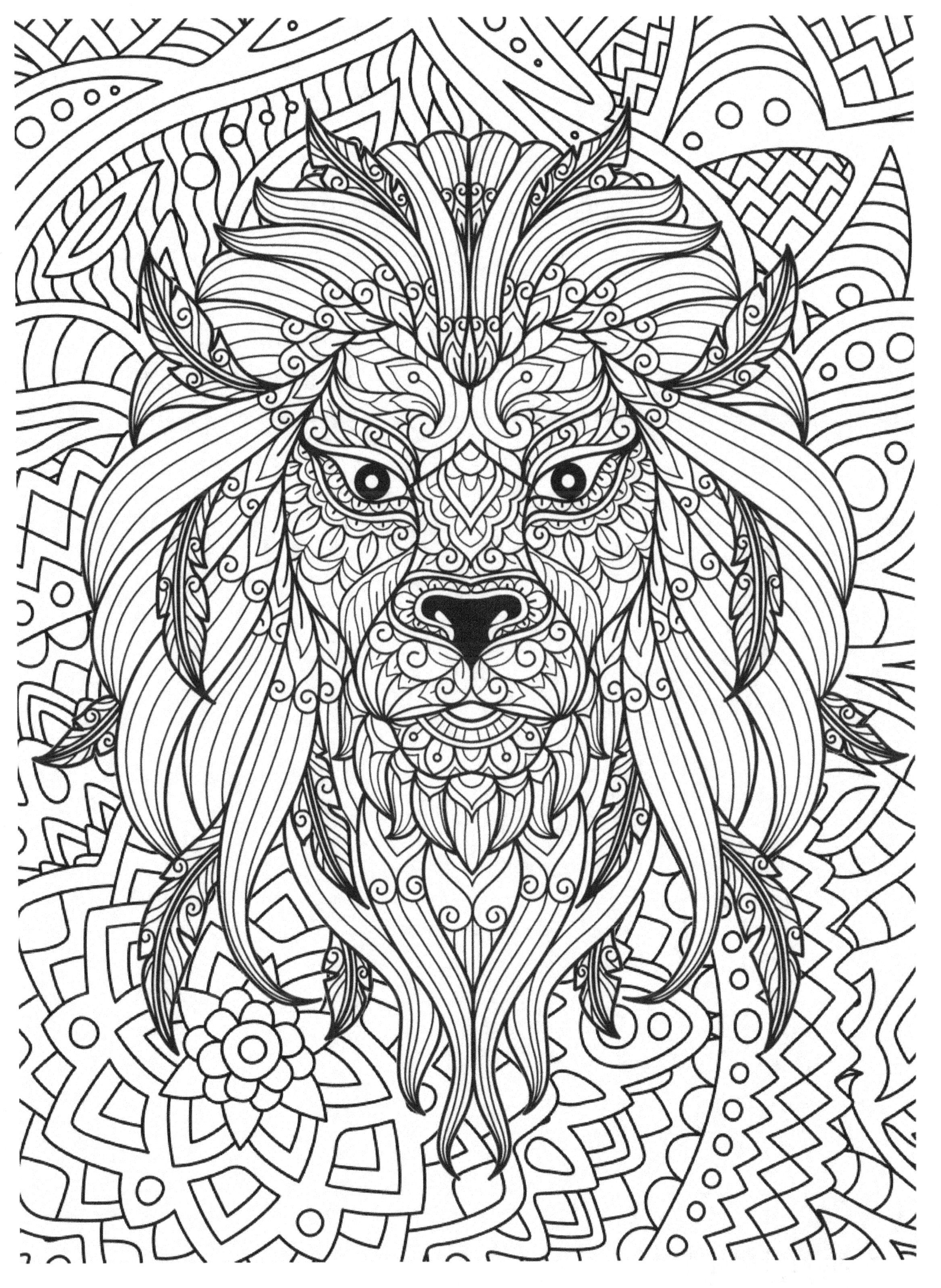